# Dynamics 365 Business Central Development Quick Start Guide

Modern development techniques for Dynamics 365 Business Central

**Stefano Demiliani**
**Duilio Tacconi**

BIRMINGHAM - MUMBAI

# Dynamics 365 Business Central Development Quick Start Guide

**Commissioning Editor:** Pavan Ramchandani
**Acquisition Editor:** Siddharth Mandal
**Content Development Editor:** Mohammed Yusuf Imaratwale
**Technical Editor:** Sushmeeta Jena
**Copy Editor:** Safis Editing
**Project Coordinator:** Nidhi Joshi
**Proofreader:** Safis Editing
**Indexer:** Tejal Daruwale Soni
**Graphics:** Jason Monteiro
**Production Coordinator:** Nilesh Mohite

First published: August 2018

Production reference: 1240818

Published by Packt Publishing Ltd.
Livery Place
35 Livery Street
Birmingham
B3 2PB, UK.

ISBN 978-1-78934-746-3

www.packtpub.com

`mapt.io`

Mapt is an online digital library that gives you full access to over 5,000 books and videos, as well as industry leading tools to help you plan your personal development and advance your career. For more information, please visit our website.

# Why subscribe?

- Spend less time learning and more time coding with practical eBooks and Videos from over 4,000 industry professionals

- Improve your learning with Skill Plans built especially for you

- Get a free eBook or video every month

- Mapt is fully searchable

- Copy and paste, print, and bookmark content

# PacktPub.com

Did you know that Packt offers eBook versions of every book published, with PDF and ePub files available? You can upgrade to the eBook version at `www.PacktPub.com` and as a print book customer, you are entitled to a discount on the eBook copy. Get in touch with us at `service@packtpub.com` for more details.

At `www.PacktPub.com`, you can also read a collection of free technical articles, sign up for a range of free newsletters, and receive exclusive discounts and offers on Packt books and eBooks.

# Contributors

## About the authors

**Stefano Demiliani** is a Microsoft MVP on business applications, a Microsoft Certified Solution Developer, and a long-time expert on different Microsoft technologies.

He has a master's degree in Computer Engineering from Politecnico of Turin, he works as a CTO for EID/Navlab (one of the main Microsoft Partners in Italy), and he has recently moved many customers around the globe onto the cloud.

He has worked with Packt Publishing on many IT books, and he's the author of *Building ERP Solutions with Microsoft Dynamics NAV* (a hands-on guide on building enterprise architectures based on the Microsoft Dynamics NAV ERP and Azure) and *Implementing Azure Cloud Design Patterns*. You can reach him on Twitter (@demiliani) or on LinkedIn.

> *We hope that this book will help you to be successful with this jump. Thanks to all the wonderful staff that has worked with me on this book (especially Duilio for consenting to be on board), and thanks also to my family (I'll return to you all the hours spent working on this project). I would like to dedicate this book to my little daughter, Sara: I love you. Maybe one day you will be proud of me for this.*

**Duilio Tacconi** is a Microsoft Dynamics NAV/Microsoft Dynamics 365 Business Central Escalation Engineer at Microsoft EMEA Customer Support and Services (CSS). He joined Microsoft in 2008 after working in a

customer IT department with a focus primarily on system administration and development.

Despite graduating with the highest score in Agricultural Science in 1996, he has been on the ERP circuit since 1998 as a developer and a system implementer for several companies with Microsoft and non-Microsoft technologies.

Currently, he is a SME at EMEA and one of Microsoft EMEA CSS references for Managed Service for Partners

Three times Iron Man finisher, Duilio lives in Cernusco Sul Naviglio (Italy) with his beloved wife, Laura, and his son, Leonardo.

> *Born with the heart and soul of Microsoft Dynamics NAV, Microsoft Dynamics 365 Business Central has all the features, tools, and power needed to dominate the SMB market over the next few decades. Thanks to all the Packt guys for all the professional help, and a warm thank you to Stefano for dragging me into this project. I dedicate this book to Laura: my love, my life, and special half.*

# About the reviewers

In 1999, Luc van Vugt stepped into the NAV world, training hundreds of developers, most of whom are still around.

After Microsoft acquired Navision, Luc joined the Dynamics localization team GDL as tester, UA specialist, and project lead. For 6 years, he was involved with all successive releases.

Since he left Microsoft, Luc has become an active community member by means of his blog, co-founder of the Dutch Dynamics Community, and a speaker at conferences. In 2014, he co-founded NAV Skills supporting NAV pros around the globe with, among others, webinars. Luc has also been awarded MS MVP since 2011.

In 2012, Luc started fluxxus.nl, doing miscellaneous projects including NAV development courses and workshops on design patterns and automated testing.

> *Next to my wife Saskia, our three great kids, and friends, who keep me growing as a human being, I would like to acknowledge Hardik Bhinde at Packt for very effective and efficient cooperation.*

**Eric** is one of the founding partners of iFacto Business Solutions and Cloud Ready Software. With his 18 years of technical expertise, he is an everyday inspiration to its development teams. As development manager, he continually acts upon the technical readiness of iFacto and CRS.Apart from that, Eric is also very active in the NAV community, where he tries to solve technical issues and shares his knowledge with other Dynamics enthusiasts. Surely, many among you will have read some of Eric's posts, which he invariably signs with waldo. Lots of people have been using and even contributing to tools he shares for free on GitHub.His proven track record entitled him to be awarded since 2007 as Microsoft MVP (Most Valuable Professional).

# Packt is searching for authors like you

If you're interested in becoming an author for Packt, please visit `authors.packtpub.com` and apply today. We have worked with thousands of developers and tech professionals, just like you, to help them share their insight with the global tech community. You can make a general application, apply for a specific hot topic that we are recruiting an author for, or submit your own idea.

# Table of Contents

# Preface

With the release of Dynamics 365 Business Central, Microsoft has changed the world of the traditional ERP. Now we have an ERP platform that's totally integrated with the Office 365 ecosystem and able to work in the cloud (SaaS) and on-premise. Dynamics 365 Business Central is a big change also in the programming model: now we have extensions and a completely new platform for development.

This book aims to be a guide on developing and deploying solutions with Dynamics 365 Business Central. It covers all the essentials of extensions development and all you need in order to create your solutions on the new ERP platform.

By the end of this book, you will have mastered Dynamics 365 Business Central solution development.

## Who this book is for

The target audience of this book is essentially the following:

- Dynamics 365 Business Central solution developers
- IT solution architects (mainly involved in implementing ERP solutions based on the Dynamics 365 Business Central platform)
- Designers of business applications

This book assumes that the readers have a working knowledge of the C/AL language and that they are able to developing solutions with C/AL and C/SIDE. A basic knowledge of C#, Visual Studio, web services, and REST protocols will be useful.

## What this book covers

Chapter 1, *Microsoft Dynamics 365 Business Central Overview*, introduces the readers to the new Microsoft SaaS ERP platform. It explains the new architecture, how it differs from the on-premise traditional ERP proposition, and the benefits of adopting a completely cloud solution.

Chapter 2, *The New Extension Model*, explains the basic concepts of the new development framework for Dynamics 365 Business Central (triggers, events), describes how it differs from the traditional programming model based on C/AL, and introduces the new concept of apps.

Chapter 3, *Modern Development Environment Overview*, describes the new programming platform for Dynamics 365 Business Central based on Visual Studio Code and the AL extension, with tips on how to customize your development environment to be more proficient when programming and how to configure the environment for developing your first extension.

Chapter 4, *Creating Your Development Sandbox*, introduces the concept of Dynamics 365 Business Central sandbox environments (cloud-based or Docker-based), introduces the concept of Docker containers, and explains how to create an environment for developing solutions with Dynamics 365 Business Central.

Chapter 5, *Developing an Extension with AL and Visual Studio Code*, describes how to develop a complete solution for Dynamics 365 Business Central by using the new AL language and Visual Studio Code. Starting from a business scenario, we develop a complete solution that creates new objects and extends the standard functionalities of Microsoft's ERP. Programming rules and many architectural concepts, such as dependencies, will be explained in this chapter.

Chapter 6, *Deploying Extensions*, describes how to deploy and debug an extension for Dynamics 365 Business Central. You will see how to debug AL code from Visual Studio Code and how to publish an extension in a sandbox environment or in a production environment.

Chapter 7, *Integration and Serverless Processing*, describes how to integrate an external solution with Dynamics 365 Business Central (by using REST API or web services), how to create service-oriented solutions with AL, and how to use other Dynamics 365 products, such as Flow and PowerApps, to create business applications that work with Dynamics 365 Business Central.

# To get the most out of this book

The readers should have a basic knowledge of the C/AL language and the old Microsoft Dynamics ERP platform (Dynamics NAV).

The readers should have a trial version of Dynamics 365 Business Central. A trial version can be activated by going to `https://trials.dynamics.com/Dynamics365/Signup/BusinessCentral`.

The readers should have Visual Studio Code installed on their local machine. Visual Studio Code can be downloaded from the following link: `https://code.visualstudio.com/download`.

# Download the example code files

You can download the example code files for this book from your account at `www.packtpub.com`. If you purchased this book elsewhere, you can visit `www.packtpub.com/support` and register to have the files emailed directly to you.

You can download the code files by following these steps:

1. Log in or register at `www.packtpub.com`.
2. Select the **SUPPORT** tab.
3. Click on **Code Downloads & Errata**.
4. Enter the name of the book in the **Search** box and follow the onscreen instructions.

Once the file is downloaded, please make sure that you unzip or extract the folder using the latest version of:

- WinRAR/7-Zip for Windows
- Zipeg/iZip/UnRarX for Mac
- 7-Zip/PeaZip for Linux

The code bundle for the book is also hosted on GitHub at `https://github.com/PacktPublishing/Dynamics-365-Business-Central-Development-Quick-Start-Guide`. In case there's an update to the code, it will be updated on the existing GitHub repository.

We also have other code bundles from our rich catalog of books and videos available at `https://github.com/PacktPublishing/`. Check them out!

# Download the color images

We also provide a PDF file that has color images of the screenshots/diagrams used in this book. You can download it here: `http://www.packtpub.com/sites/default/files/downloads/Dynamics365BusinessCentralDevelopmentQuickStartGuide_ColorImages.pdf`.

# Conventions used

There are a number of text conventions used throughout this book.

`CodeInText`: Indicates code words in text, database table names, folder names, filenames, file extensions, pathnames, dummy URLs, user input, and Twitter handles. Here is an example: "Mount the downloaded `WebStorm-10*.dmg` disk image file as another disk in your system."

A block of code is set as follows:

```
finsql.exe Command=generatesymbolreference, Database="Demo Database NAV
(11-0)", ServerName=NAVSRV
```

When we wish to draw your attention to a particular part of a code block, the relevant lines or items are set in bold:

```
// Example:
// "Print to console": {
//   "prefix": "log",
//   "body": [
//       "console.log('$1');",
//       "$2
//   ],
//   "description": "Log output to console"
```

Any command-line input or output is written as follows:

```
docker ps
```

**Bold**: Indicates a new term, an important word, or words that you see onscreen. For example, words in menus or dialog boxes appear in the text like this. Here is an example: "Select **System info** from the **Administration** panel."

Warnings or important notes appear like this.

Tips and tricks appear like this.

# Get in touch

Feedback from our readers is always welcome.

**General feedback**: Email `feedback@packtpub.com` and mention the book title in the subject of your message. If you have questions about any aspect of this book, please email us at `questions@packtpub.com`.

**Errata**: Although we have taken every care to ensure the accuracy of our content, mistakes do happen. If you have found a mistake in this book, we would be grateful if you would report this to us. Please visit `www.packtpub.com/submit-errata`, selecting your book, clicking on the Errata Submission Form link, and entering the details.

**Piracy**: If you come across any illegal copies of our works in any form on the Internet, we would be grateful if you would provide us with the location address or website name. Please contact us at `copyright@packtpub.com` with a link to the material.

**If you are interested in becoming an author**: If there is a topic that you have expertise in and you are interested in either writing or contributing to a book, please visit `authors.packtpub.com`.

# Reviews

Please leave a review. Once you have read and used this book, why not leave a review on the site that you purchased it from? Potential readers can then see and use your unbiased opinion to make purchase decisions, we at Packt can understand what you think about our products, and our authors can see your feedback on their book. Thank you!

For more information about Packt, please visit `packtpub.com`.

# Microsoft Dynamics 365 Business Central Overview

1

 Microsoft Dynamics 365 Business Central is a cloud-based **Enterprise Resource Planning** (**ERP**) application delivered with the **Software as a Service** (**SaaS**) model through **Cloud Solution Provider** (**CSP**) certified partners.

It is part of the Microsoft Dynamics 365 suite (the Microsoft proposition for a new generation of intelligent and integrated business applications) that includes in its portfolio **Customer Relationship Management** (**CRM**) and **ERP** software.

In this chapter, we will cover the following topics:

- What Microsoft Dynamics 365 Business Central is, what functional areas it covers, and its prices
- A history of the Microsoft ERP offering evolution for small to medium-sized businesses, (SMB) in the cloud
- An overview of Microsoft Dynamics 365 Business Central architecture
- On-premises versus SaaS-based deployments

## Introducing Microsoft Dynamics 365 Business Central

The current Microsoft Dynamics 365 family portfolio could be described as follows.

Here is some information regarding the ERP cloud-based version:

- **Microsoft Dynamics 365 Business Central**: This targets small to medium-sized businesses. The product has a solid and strong Microsoft Azure footprint. Its application and some core technologies come from a streamlined evolution of Microsoft Dynamics NAV. This has been a well-known market leader in the SMB ERP software segment for the last 30 years.
- **Microsoft Dynamics 365 for Financials & Operations**: This targets enterprise businesses. It represents the transformation equivalent of another historical Microsoft product: Microsoft Dynamics AX.

CRM cloud-based and specific ERP modules offer the following:

- Microsoft Dynamics 365 for Sales
- Microsoft Dynamics 365 for Customer Service
- Microsoft Dynamics 365 for Field Service
- Microsoft Dynamics 365 for Project Automation
- Microsoft Dynamics 365 for Retail
- Microsoft Dynamics 365 for Talent
- Microsoft Dynamics 365 for Marketing

For each of these products, Microsoft provides partner and customer full official documentation at the following link: `https://dynamics.microsoft.com/`.

To subscribe to a fast setup of Microsoft Dynamics 365 Business Central, start with the trial version; everyone around the world simply needs a suitable work email linked to an Office 365 subscription and a phone number. Just follow this link: `https://trials.dynamics.com/Dynamics365/Signup/BusinessCentral`.

While trials are open to everyone, when the trial period ends, the product needs to be purchased. Customer official licensing is assigned exclusively through Microsoft partners that are credited and certified by the CSP program.

Microsoft Dynamics 365 Business Central delivers out-of-the-box functionalities in modules with a fixed price per month, per user licence model. The SaaS version is quite simple, and there are basically two licence types of user choices, with different capabilities:

- **ESSENTIALS (currently from $70 per month)**:
    - Financial management
    - Customer-relationship management
    - Project management

- Supply-chain management
- Human-resource management
- Warehouse management

- **PREMIUM (currently from $100 per month)**:
  - All included in ESSENTIALS
  - Service management
  - Manufacturing

More details about licensing types and their benefits are described in the official Microsoft Dynamics 365 Business Central Licensing Guide: `https://go.microsoft.com/fwlink/?LinkId=871590clcid=0x409`.

Once you get started with your trial or production version, you will be offered a productive, intuitive, and user-friendly web client interface:

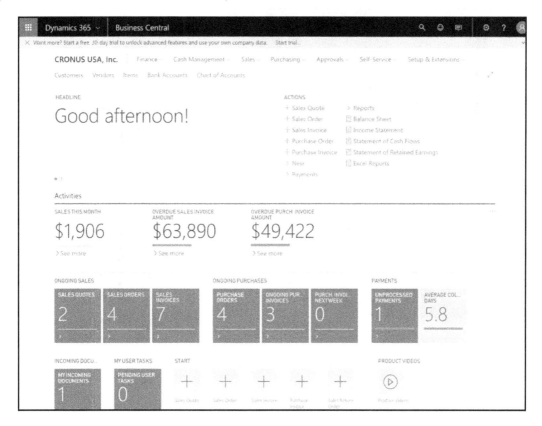

Web client interface

The Microsoft Dynamics 365 Business Central web client is supported by the following browsers:

- Microsoft Edge
- Internet Explorer 11 or higher
- Google Chrome 61.0 for Windows or higher
- Mozilla Firefox 55.0 for Windows or higher
- Safari 10.0 for macOS or higher

While the best experience is offered by the latest Microsoft technologies (Microsoft Edge), Microsoft Dynamics 365 Business Central can also be deployed to almost every device, such as tablets or phones, by downloading an app (technically known as a universal app) from the main marketplaces: Windows Store, Google Play, and Apple Store (`https://docs.microsoft.com/en-us/dynamics365/business-central/install-mobile-app`):

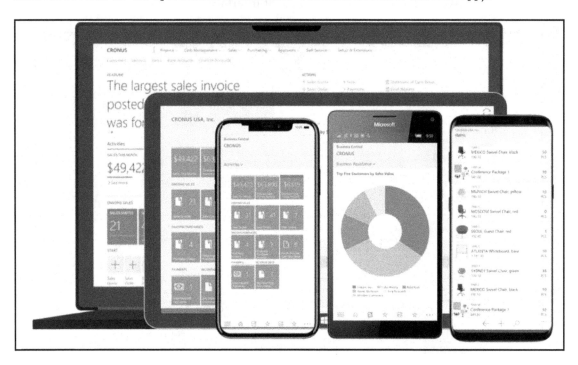

Different devices where Microsoft Dynamics 365 Business Central can be deployed

Currently, Microsoft Dynamics 365 Business Central is localized and released in the following countries:

- United States
- Canada
- United Kingdom
- Denmark
- Netherlands
- Germany
- Spain
- Italy
- France
- Austria
- Switzerland
- Belgium
- Sweden
- Finland
- Australia
- New Zealand

In the fall of 2018, it will also be localized and available in these countries:

- Iceland
- Mexico
- Norway

Since the Microsoft Dynamics 365 Business Central July 2018 update, it is also possible for partners to create their own localized versions, starting from the **worldwide standard application base** (called **W1**) and distributed as an app through the Microsoft Dynamics 365 marketplace called **AppSource.** For more informations, you can check the following link:

```
https://docs.microsoft.com/en-us/dynamics365/business-central/dev-itpro/
developer/readiness/readiness-develop-localization).
```

The first two countries being localized externally by partner through extension (the new programming model that we'll see in this book), available through AppSource, are the following ones:

- United Arab Emirates (UAE)
- South Africa
- South Korea

Here you can see an example of the South Korea localization:

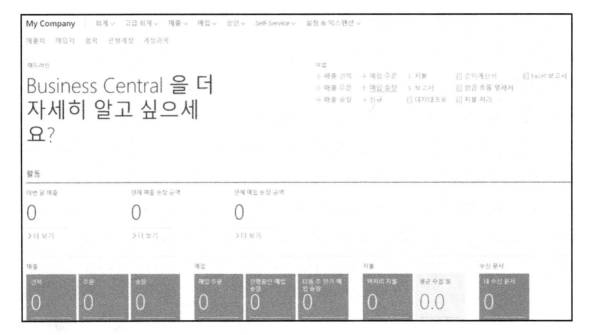

Many more localized versions have been announced to be released as extensions (SaaSified) from the partner channel in fall 2018 update.

# A brief history of the Microsoft Dynamics cloud-based ERP SMB product

Microsoft Dynamics 365 Business Central is the evolved form of Microsoft Dynamics NAV (formerly known as Navision). This is a worldwide ERP market-leading product in the SMB segment. In this paragraph, we will explore the timeline of this product, focusing on its latest releases as well as its cloud journey:

- **1983**: The native company (PC & C A/S) was founded in 1983. *Navision* ERP solution was released in 1987 and had an exponential technical evolution that culminated in the 1995 Microsoft Windows version release. This release consisted of a greatly improved platform.
- **2002**: The astonishing evolution of Navision—both in terms of application module add-ons and technology enrichment - led Microsoft to finalize the acquisition of Navision and its channel in 2002. This was one of the most prolific technological marriages of the 21st century. Later, this converged as a unified business, offering a stack called Microsoft Dynamics.
- **2007**: During this year, Navision changed its name to Microsoft Dynamics NAV.

During the on-premises ERP boom, Microsoft Dynamics offered a complete business suite. This was targeted at all needs and fully covered the requirements of enterprise (Microsoft Dynamics AX), SMB (Microsoft Dynamics NAV) ERP application, and CRM (Microsoft Dynamics CRM).

- **October 2008**: The Microsoft Dynamics NAV development team changed the old two-tier client–server technology in favor of a more scalable and performant three-tier technology. This change isolated main business logic, executed through a **Windows Communication Framework** (**WCF**) service called Microsoft Dynamics NAV Server, from a data tier to a client tier.
- **November 2012**: With Microsoft Dynamics NAV 2013, the old C++ Classic Client was deprecated, relegating it to development purposes only. It completed its transformation into a fully memory managed stack based on a solid 64-bit WCF service that operated with both a WinForm based Windows Client and a brand new ASP.NET Web Client. This unleashed the potential of all native .NET Framework based Microsoft technologies and their versatile and flexible implementations and integrations.

- **November 2013**: The cloud journey of Microsoft Dynamics NAV reached its very first milestone with the release of Microsoft Dynamics NAV 2013 R2. With the support of Infrastructure as a Service's (IaaS) deployment in Microsoft Azure Virtual Machines (VMs), Microsoft Dynamics NAV 2013 R2 was equipped with an entire set of Windows PowerShell scripts called **Microsoft Dynamics NAV Provisioning Tools.** These tools were designed to completely manage the deployment, configuration and setup for Microsoft Dynamics NAV on Microsoft Azure.

Microsoft Dynamics NAV 2013 R2 was also referred to as the first version to support multitenancy, typically used in private or public hosting environments where a single WCF service could work on several data tenants bound to the same application.

Worldwide interest in all kinds of enterprises for cloud-based deployment led the Microsoft Dynamics stack to quickly evolve and embrace this type of deployment.

- **November 2014**: At this point, Microsoft Dynamics NAV 2015 supports the Microsoft Azure SQL database. This is an enhanced web client experience and a brand new universal app targeted at tablet devices, and downloadable from the most well-known marketplaces, including the Windows Store, Google Play, and the Apple store.

From that time, many customers dropped their local infrastructure in favor of a cloud-based one. Today, Microsoft Dynamics NAV partners use Microsoft Azure as the hosting environment for their own portfolios.

Microsoft recognized this as just the first (r)evolutionary step in the modernization and transformation of the cloud product.

- **November 2015**: A year later, Microsoft Dynamics NAV 2016 reached **general availability (GA)**. In terms of development, this was a game-changer.

This was the first version to implement event publishing and subscription as well as being able to isolate custom development into modules, leading to a zero footprint change in the standard base application code. The official release of this version was not only capable of isolating custom code changes, but it could also create seamless packages called extensions. These extensions were designed to improve the application experience at runtime. Extensions can be installed, published, unpublished, and uninstalled like any modern app you may have on your phone or any other connected device; the logic behind all of these factors is the same.

Microsoft Dynamics NAV 2016 was also a game-changing version in terms of deployment types.

Universal apps in marketplaces and stores were updated to support both tablet and phone devices, leading to a full immersive user experience in the most widely used devices in the world.

Microsoft Dynamics NAV can now be deployed in Windows OS-based PCs with a fully fledged windows client. It can also be accessed through a web browser as a web client, or even installed and used in tablets or phones as an app.

The cloud version of Microsoft Dynamics NAV was also a game-changer.

Microsoft Dynamics NAV was also offered as a **Platform as a Service** (**PaaS**) solution to its partners. The Microsoft Dynamics NAV PaaS offering was named **Managed Service for Partners** (**MSfP**). More information can be found here: `https://mbs.microsoft.com/` `partnersource/global/sales-marketing/marketing-collateral/messaging-frameworks/` `NAVmanagedservice`.

MSfP is accessed through a secure web portal based on Microsoft Dynamics NAV web client. Here, selected partners can develop their private **Intellectual Property** (**IP**) customizations on premises. When modifications are certified and committed, the database that contains the customizations is split into an application tier and a data tier. Furthermore, two different bacpacs (Microsoft Azure SQL backup) are uploaded into the MSfP portal, creating the main branch for that specific customer, also known as the main or first application version.

MSfP portal is equipped with several pages and actions that allow the user to create an entire cloud-based infrastructure deployment with both a web client and a windows client offering for end users:

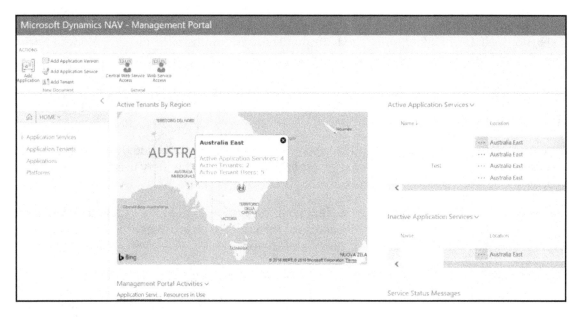

Microsoft Dynamics NAV- Management Portal

With just a couple of clicks, an entire Microsoft Dynamics NAV infrastructure can be created from scratch. Users will then receive a (customizable) welcome email containing links for connecting to the Microsoft Dynamics NAV web client from any device. They will also be given a link to automatically download and install Microsoft Dynamics NAV windows client through ClickOnce-based technology.

Tenant databases are periodically moved to an upgraded application service from one that has a specific Microsoft Dynamics NAV platform **Cumulative Update** (**CU**) applied. This typically happens around every three months.

At the moment, customers who started with Microsoft Dynamics NAV 2016 are now happily running Microsoft Dynamics NAV 2018 with the latest CU applied, both technically and at application level.

The PaaS architecture proposition represents another milestone reached in the history of Microsoft Dynamics NAV. This was also the next huge advancement of the cloud: a SaaS-based offering.

- **April 2016**: Here, Microsoft announced *Project Madeira*: the nickname for another branch of the Microsoft Dynamics NAV application. This was mainly intended to be used by accountants through web client access and sold directly or through CSP partners under the SaaS formula. The infrastructure was clearly an evolution of the PaaS structure, as the application starts its own metamorphosis and changes to accommodate a more simple and user-friendly experience.

Project Madeira only supported the essential and simplified basic financial part of the Microsoft Dynamics NAV application, completely excluding service and manufacturing features.

- **November 2016**: Project Madeira was officially renamed as Microsoft Dynamics 365 for Financials and GA in the United States and Canada only. At the same time, on-premise Microsoft Dynamics NAV 2017 was released.
- **April 2017**: Microsoft Dynamics 365 for Financials again changed its name to Microsoft Dynamics 365 for Financials and Operations: Business Edition. Together with United States and Canada, it was also localized and released in the United Kingdom.
- **November 2017**: In November 2017, the Microsoft Dynamics NAV 2018 on-premises version was released with hybrid development. This included the old legacy CSIDE development environment as well as a new language and modern development environment which was deployed through an extension for Visual Studio Code (`.vsix`). This hybrid development intended to accelerate the transition from the current traditional customization paradigm into the modern extensibility concept. Creating an extension is currently the only development model for SaaS-based deployments.
- **April 2018**: Microsoft Dynamics 365 Business Central is GA in 14 countries. It was also presented as the evolution of the Microsoft Dynamics NAV software which was predicted to have a bright future in the cloud.

All Microsoft Dynamics 365 for Financials and Operations: Business Edition tenants are now moved to Business Central, and the term is officially archived and deprecated by Microsoft. Microsoft Dynamics 365 Business Central is the equivalent of a fully-fledged Microsoft Dynamics NAV web client application but it is distributed as a SaaS offering through CSP partners.

Furthermore, AppSource is now the marketplace where **Independent Software Vendors (ISVs)**, **Value Added Resellers (VARs)** and credited partners submit certified app extensions that can be published and installed by partners and customers in order to enrich the application. AppSource is also the gathering point used to promote partner consultant services. More information can be found here: `https://appsource.microsoft.com/en-us/marketplace/apps?page=1product=dynamics-365-business-central`.

- **Fall 2018**: The next appointment in this exciting cloud evolution is set to be November 2018. This will be the release of the Dynamics 365 Business Central enhanced fall update and also the release of the on-premise Dynamics 365 Business Central version. To find out more about the Fall 2018 update, please visit this address: `https://docs.microsoft.com/en-us/business-applications-release-notes/October18/dynamics365-business-central/`.

# Microsoft Dynamics 365 Business Central Architecture

Multi tenancy is the key technology that makes Microsoft Dynamics 365 Business Central very flexible and scalable. Wrapped around multi tenancy, there are several of the latest Microsoft Azure-featured technologies that provide support for different logical software layers (tiers).

Since the Microsoft Corporation is committed to and focused on being the worldwide leader in cloud technologies, expect Microsoft Dynamics 365 Business Central to change and evolve quickly in its architecture design, as did its glorious predecessor Microsoft Dynamics NAV, in the coming decades. This continuous technological update of both platform and application could lead the product to fast and exponentially grow in the ERP SMB market, years after years.

As cloud technologies are by definition always up to date, what is discussed in this chapter might be evolved by the time you are reading it. However, with high degrees of chances, the logical concept of software layer isolation will remain unchanged and a pillar to build cloud services.

- **Database Tier**: Every single Microsoft Dynamics 365 Business Central customer tenant, production, or sandbox, is a single Microsoft Azure SQL database. Together with customer tenant databases, there are few application databases used to store application objects and system tables that are mounted on a Microsoft Dynamics 365 Business Central Server service. This service is used to share and serve several different tenant databases with the same application code base. Tenant databases are periodically dismounted from an outdated service, in terms of platform and application, and mounted to the latest one, with a close to zero downtime for end users and a transparent continuous upgrade and product evolution. Azure SQL Databases are managed and scaled using elastic pool. More informations here: `https://docs.microsoft.com/en-us/azure/sql-database/sql-database-elastic-pool`

- **Service Tier**: Also known as the Application Service tier, it is a set of Azure VM(s) where Microsoft Dynamics 365 Business Central Service and Web Server components are installed. Microsoft Dynamics 365 Business Central Service connects and handles process calls from customer tenant bounded to the same application base. Azure VMs are load balanced, to easily distribute horizontally the process execution load. Logically, the service tier is built-in as a Microsoft Azure Service Fabric Cluster where several Azure resources and features are combined for a fast, redundant, secure, and repeatable creation of application services. More information here: `https://docs.microsoft.com/en-us/azure/service-fabric/service-fabric-overview`. To give just a quick example of the feature used, the Azure Application Gateway is extensively adopted for endpoint monitoring and cluster load balancing. Each Microsoft Azure Fabric Cluster is equipped with all the resources and features needed to cope with scalability and high service availability. All technologies making of a cluster are always up to date. To give you another quick example, Azure VMs currently run the Microsoft Windows Server 2016, fully patched.

Both database and service tiers are constantly monitored to guarantee service health and availability. Collecting data and its further automated processing falls under the *Telemetry* term.

Telemetry is enabled at every level with Microsoft Dynamics 365 Business Central. If an application service or database tier reports any kind of warning or error, this is quickly sent to service operation teams that quickly react to it and guarantee a class-A uptime **service level agreement** (**SLA**) to all users.

Telemetry applies to the infrastructure artifacts and to the application logic. The Microsoft Dynamics 365 Business Central service emits logs that traces activities, and telemetry is capable of catching application-driven errors that are submitted to the relevant application team. The application team corrects application issues that will be included in the latest application tenant spin ups, together with feature enhancements. This will guarantee a solid, robust, and smooth product evolution.

Telemetry emits terabytes of data in a few weeks, and it is constantly under automated or on-demand analysis, and its outcome is used to improve and strengthen both the platform and the application efficiently.

Data generation and analysis is performed with the highest possible level of security guaranteed by the Microsoft Corporation. To provide an example, only certified and elected Microsoft service engineers can access infrastructure modules, and this is done only through specific, certified **secure administration workstations** (**SAW**). More informations here: `https://msdn.microsoft.com/en-us/library/mt186538.aspx`.

All in all, Microsoft Dynamics 365 Business Central represents the best-in-class solution for ERP SaaS applications and the result of current and future profitable infrastructural investment made by the Microsoft Corporation in the SMB segment.

# On-premises versus cloud-based deployment

Both Microsoft Dynamics NAV and Microsoft Dynamics 365 Business Central have roughly the same application base, hence share the very same feature capabilities. What changes in the equation, then, is the deployment type: on-premises versus SaaS.

The first question that an IT manager in this context faces is: should we go on premises or embrace the cloud? Normally, an ERP application is a core software part for a company, and this decision could drastically affect business processes at all levels and influence decision makers. It represents the vital heart of a company and it is crucial in guaranteeing its prosperous future. Let's try to compare both types of product deployments to better understand the pros and cons and find a duly qualified answer to the question.

# Infrastructure costs, maintenance, and availability

Microsoft Dynamics NAV requires consistent initial investments to purchase or rent, if hosted, the required redundant hardware and software to guarantee high availability and a smooth daily activity. Moreover, it needs experienced IT staff to manage the whole system deployment monolith.

Once the system is fully functional, it also needs to be maintained. From time to time, the entire hardware will need to be upgraded, and additional software will also need to be added.

Keep in mind that a Microsoft life cycle has typically an on-premises mainstream life cycle of five years. After that period, Microsoft products have an extra five years of limited support (out of mainstream), where it is not possible anymore to enable the escalation chain to the relevant development team and only security hotfixes are guaranteed. After five years, then, Microsoft warmly suggests that the partner and the customer upgrade to the latest version.

With Microsoft Dynamics 365 Business Central, there is no initial deployment cost. With the pay-as-you-go offering philosophy, customers simply have to choose, according to their business needs, an essential and/or premium user experience, depending on the application modules they need.

There is no need to take care of any hardware maintenance: Microsoft guarantees the underlying software to run on the latest technologies and fully patched with a close to zero or no downtime at all, and with a class-A uptime SLA.

# Security

Companies that store data internally, on-premises, have complete control over it in terms of accessibility (read) and maintenance (insert, update, delete) rights. But great power comes with great responsibility. IT departments are responsible to guarantee the appropriate privacy and respect their own, local, and legal rules. In Europe, the recent **General Data Protection Regulation** (**GDPR**) defines clearly how to rank and handle it. This is a cost for all companies that are requested today to implement, maintain and monitor those rules in all business processes.

The same applies to the hosting environment: if you are delivering a hosting service, then you have to update your business process and enpower your staff to cope with security and legally guarantee the security level requested, at least, by the current laws in your country. If you are the CEO, CFO, or IT manager of a company that uses outsourced hosting services for your ERP, then you have probably signed an SLA where your hosting provider guarantees the security of your own data. The cost of the service is higher according to the level of security.

There are no companies in the world that can guarantee the highest service SLA guaranteed by Microsoft Cloud security policies offered with Microsoft Dynamics 365 Business Central. Being a cloud service (always up to date), it is already compliant with all the regulations of the countries where it is deployed, included in the GDPR. There is no extra cost to pay.

## Performances

With Microsoft Dynamics NAV, performance is the responsibility of the implementor, unless the cause is to be found in the standard application. In this case, Microsoft needs to respond and provide a hotfix or guidance regarding how to resolve it.

As a partner or customer, you might make your own decision to choose whatever hardware resources you want, according to your budget. As a partner or customer, you might change whatever configuration parameter in your Microsoft SQL Server or Microsoft Dynamics NAV Server and/or decide to customize the application in its core to be tailored perfectly and tightly to your business needs and growth pace.

One of the biggest advantages of Microsoft Dynamics NAV, compared to all the other ERP products in the world: It is open to almost every kind of customization and uses an object-based language that's pretty simple to learn and master.

But, with great power comes great responsibility.

If your hardware resource implementation and/or your configuration settings and/or custom application code changes bring the overall application to slow down, in terms of performance, compared to the baseline, then it is also your duty to investigate, troubleshoot, and mitigate the issue.

You break it, you fix it.

The Microsoft Dynamics 365 Business Central, as all modern SaaS propositions, comes with a fully tested standard application targeted for the SMB load. So, what is the SMB load? There is no rule of thumb but just a raw and simple definition for the SMB territory, from a marketing perspective, which is described like a business application used by 1 up to 250 users. This broad marketing concept does not appropriately match with objective technical considerations. Most probably, the definition could or should potentially be changed in favor of *a number of transactions, per unit of time*. But also this measure, in some circumstances, could be not enough to let stakeholders decide what hardware to buy and which configuration to apply.

Microsoft Dynamics 365 Business Central comes equipped with a very high technology telemetry implemented at all software and hardware levels. The Microsoft operation service engineers could quickly determine whether there are performance issues, whether these are hardware or software based, whether these affect single or multiple tenants, and in a short time determine the root cause of these and mitigate them, at the required cloud speed.

If the root cause is not isolated but potentially applies to all tenants (for example, a missing database index or a suboptimal code), then this will be ported to the application or infrastructure and in the next iteration, also known as a tenant update, so that all the customers will clearly benefit from this.

# Scalability

On-premises installations require today highly specialized projects to design the current hardware infrastructure to cope with the contingent business process needs and the consequent data load and its periodicity or seasonality.

Since projects might start several months before they go live, and typically SMB companies are very flexible and adapt fast, at the moment production starts, the business conditions and the data transaction quality and quantity might have been changed. Then, the project stakeholders have to tweak and tune the infrastructure configuration by changing this at different levels: application (code changes), infrastructure (configurations), and hardware (add more resources). Scalability of resources is crucial for SMB ERP, and it requires time to implement the right strategy at the right time, and it is an ever-changing dynamic process.

Microsoft Dynamics 365 Business Central uses the full power of the Microsoft Azure cloud, and telemetry could detect all types of needs at once. Scalability and resource economy is in the nature of the SaaS-based solution.

# Upgrades

With Microsoft Dynamics NAV architecture, partners and customers have complete control over infrastructure and application upgrades. They might decide when and what to apply, and how they want to apply it. It is trivial to say that the cost of upgrade, in terms of project analysis for staging and production, resource and time allocation, and so on is the upon partner and customer.

Microsoft Dynamics 365 Business Central allows partners and customers to focus on the application business process and their daily activities.

Hardware and software upgrades are continuous within a periodical cadence. Currently, featured application updates happen roughly every three months, but these dates are not set in stone; they fluctuate. Typically, this happens in a transparent way, with zero downtime for end users.

# Customizations

In the On-Premise Microsoft Dynamics NAV there is still Classic CSIDE Development Environment available to change the standard code, together with the Modern Development Environment that consists of an Extension (VSIX) for Visual Studio Code. Almost all the On Premises installation base for Microsoft Dynamics NAV is customized using Classic Development through CSIDE with more deeper and deeper changes in the standard application, depending on specific business needs.

The classic development comes with very high flexibility and gives partners and customers more freedom when it comes to an end product that deeply satisfies customer requirements and fits like a glove around the company IT core application and integrations.

Microsoft Dynamics 365 Business Central uses only the modern development paradigm through the creation of business extensions validated by Microsoft and uploaded in the AppSource marketplace. Modern development for SaaS-based solutions does not allow for the making of any core changes to the standard application, but simply extends it.

At the moment, there are still pretty a discrete number of restrictions and limitations when it comes to providing a SaaSified solution for Microsoft Dynamics 365 Business Central, compared to the equivalent classic development.

Even as I write this, the Microsoft Dynamics 365 Business Central development team is working to reduce the gap between the classic and modern development types and guarantees partner and **independent software vendors** (ISVs) a smooth and fast transition between the two, to let AppSource grow quickly in a number of available vertical solutions, add-ons, and localizations.

We will have a deep dive in customizations in a later chapter.

## User experience

Another point in favor of on premises Microsoft Dynamics NAV is the capability to choose between windows or web client deployment. Windows client represents the evolution of the Navision Classic Client. Deployed for the first time in October 2008 as a *role tailored client* with Microsoft Dynamics NAV 2009, it has been heavily refactored and enriched during the past 10 years.

Thanks to its great features, capability, tailored user experience, and productivity, it represents today the vast majority of the client type deployment for Microsoft Dynamics NAV installations.

Despite being a valid and lightweight deployment type, the web client still has its own feature and browser limitations. These are described here: `https://docs.microsoft.com/en-us/dynamics-nav/feature-limitations-of-the-microsoft-dynamics-nav-web-client`.

Microsoft Dynamics 365 Business Central, today, can only be accessed through a web client using the most common web browsers or deployed as an app on phone or tablet devices.

Even while I write this, the Microsoft Dynamics 365 Business Central development team is working to reduce the feature limitations and gaps between the Windows and the web client and improve its productivity.

## Summary

In the very first part of this chapter, we learned what Microsoft Dynamics 365 Business Central is, its offering target, and its proposed value.

In the second part of this chapter, we covered the main features of Microsoft Dynamics 365, and looked at its architecture.

We also compared on-premises and SaaSified deployments.

In `Chapter 2`, *The New Extension Model*, we'll see the new extension model for customizing and developing solutions with Microsoft Dynamics 365 Business Central.

# The New Extension Model 2

In the previous chapter, we saw an overview of the new Microsoft Dynamics 365 Business Central platform (the new Microsoft SaaS ERP proposition), from a user to a technical perspective.

In this chapter, we'll see an overview of the new extension model for developing solutions with Microsoft Dynamics 365 Business Central.

Here, you will learn the following:

- The basics of the new extension model
- The differences between traditional customizations versus extensions
- The event programming model in Dynamics 365 Business Central

## Traditional Microsoft Dynamics NAV customizations

With the old-fashioned Microsoft Dynamics NAV ERP (on-premise proposition by Microsoft), the traditional way for customizing the solution is to use the C/SIDE and C/AL languages.

C/SIDE is the standard **integrated development environment** (IDE) born with the first versions of Microsoft Dynamics NAV. With C/SIDE and the development environment application, you have access to all the NAV objects, and from here you can customize every part of the application:

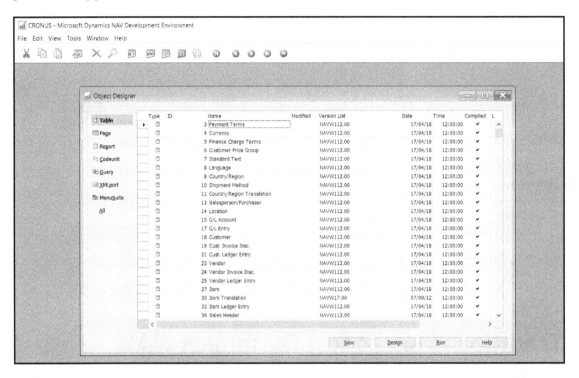

With C/SIDE and by using the C/AL language, you can create new objects such as **Tables**, **Pages**, **Codeunits** and so on and you can edit standard objects (made by Microsoft) and modify them as to your needs.

With this traditional way of programming, you can write code in new objects and you can write code inside standard objects and inside standard Microsoft code (between lines). Isolation of customizations depends only on how the developer has written their code; there are no rules and barriers when it comes to that.

For example, I can add a field to the `Customer` table called `Check Customer` with a `Boolean` type:

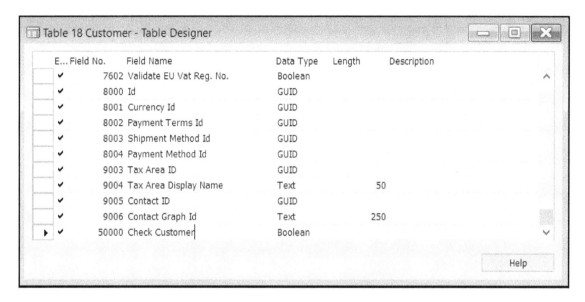

Then, I can add this field to the `Customer Card` page.

Now, if `Check Customer` flag is checked on `Customer Card`, I want a custom piece of code to start.

There are different ways of doing that, and this affects the impact of my custom code on the traditional standard Microsoft objects.

I could write my code in the `OnValidate` trigger of the `Check Customer` field in the `Customer` table:

```
977  ⊟Check Customer - OnValidate()
978   IF "Check Customer" THEN
979   BEGIN
980     //Custom code goes here...
981   END;
982
983  ⊟Check Customer - OnLookup()
984
```

Or, if I'm a very bad programmer, I could write the code directly in the `Customer Card` page:

```
Page 21 Customer Card - C/AL Editor
275  Check Customer - OnValidate()
276  IF "Check Customer" THEN
277  BEGIN
278    //Custom code goes here...
279  END;
280
281
```

Regarding a customization of a process, I can write code inside Microsoft's standard processes. For example, I can open `Codeunit 80 Sales-Post` and write custom code where I need it:

```
Codeunit 80 Sales-Post - C/AL Editor
49  EverythingInvoiced := TRUE;
50
51  // Lines
52  SalesLine.RESET;
53  SalesLine.SETRANGE("Document Type",SalesHeader."Document Type");
54  SalesLine.SETRANGE("Document No.",SalesHeader."No.");
55
56  //My custom piece of code
57  Customer.GET(SalesHeader."Sell-to Customer No.");
58  IF Customer."Check Customer" THEN
59  BEGIN
60    //Custom code goes here...
61  END;
62
63  OnBeforePostLines(SalesLine,SalesHeader,SuppressCommit);
64
65  LineCount := 0;
66  RoundingLineInserted := FALSE;
67  MergeSaleslines(SalesHeader,SalesLine,TempPrepaymentSalesLine,TempCombinedSalesLine);
68  AdjustFinalInvWith100PctPrepmt(TempCombinedSalesLine);
69
70  TempVATAmountLineRemainder.DELETEALL;
```

As you can imagine, in the traditional way, we are totally free to do what we want in the way we want.

This guarantees a total flexibility of the product (we can customize every single aspect of the application and of the business process), but in this way we have a product that, after many customization for a customer, becomes a product that is difficult to manage and difficult to upgrade to a new version.

The upgrade process is maybe the main critical aspect of a traditional Microsoft Dynamics NAV implementation. When a new version of the product comes out, if you want to upgrade to that version, you need to carefully detect all your customizations in your database and merge the modified objects. This merge operation is often performed manually, and this affects the time and costs of a migration (this is why many customers are still on the old version of the product and they've not yet planned an upgrade).

We can see a representation of a traditional customization in the following diagram:

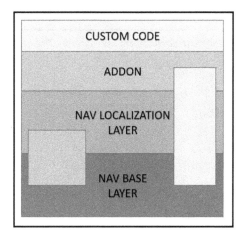

Here, we see that in a traditional Microsoft Dynamics NAV implementation we have Microsoft's base layer and Microsoft's localization layer (customizations for a specific localization). Then, we can have add-ons and we can have specific customizations for the customers. The customized code of a layer can affect the code on the other layers: an add-on can have code that affects standard localized objects and standard base objects, while a customer's customization can affect the base layer, the localization objects, and also the add-on objects.

# Triggers versus Events

All the objects in Microsoft Dynamics NAV (from the first version of the product) have **triggers**.

**Triggers** are predefined functions inside an object that are automatically executed when certain actions occur on the object itself. The body of this function could be empty (no actions required) or could contain code (that is automatically executed when the trigger occurs). Defining C/AL code in triggers allows you to change the default behavior of Microsoft Dynamics NAV.

As an example, if we open the Customer table, we can see that we have triggers for the table object (OnInsert, OnModify, OnDelete, OnRename) and triggers for the different table fields (OnValidate, OnLookup):

```
CRONUS - Microsoft Dynamics NAV Development Environment - [Table 18 Customer - C/AL Editor]
File  Edit  View  Tools  Window  Help

   1 ⊟Documentation()
   2 |
   3 ⊞OnInsert()|...
  26 ⊞OnModify()...
  38 ⊞OnDelete()...
 166 ⊞OnRename()...
 175 ⊞No. - OnValidate()...
 184 ⊞No. - OnLookup()...
 186 ⊞Name - OnValidate()...
 190 ⊟Name - OnLookup()
 191 |
 192 ⊟Search Name - OnValidate()
 193 |
 194 ⊟Search Name - OnLookup()
```

If we open the OnInsert trigger, we can see standard code in it:

```
CRONUS - Microsoft Dynamics NAV Development Environment - [Table 18 Customer - C/AL Editor]
File  Edit  View  Tools  Window  Help

 1  ⊟Documentation()
 2
 3  ⊟OnInsert()
 4  IF "No." = '' THEN BEGIN
 5    SalesSetup.GET;
 6    SalesSetup.TESTFIELD("Customer Nos.");
 7    NoSeriesMgt.InitSeries(SalesSetup."Customer Nos.",xRec."No. Series",0D,"No.","No. Series");
 8  END;
 9
10  IF "Invoice Disc. Code" = '' THEN
11    "Invoice Disc. Code" := "No.";
12
13  IF NOT (InsertFromContact OR (InsertFromTemplate AND (Contact <> '')) OR ISTEMPORARY) THEN
14    UpdateContFromCust.OnInsert(Rec);
15
16  IF "Salesperson Code" = '' THEN
17    SetDefaultSalesperson;
18
19  DimMgt.UpdateDefaultDim(
20    DATABASE::Customer,"No.",
21    "Global Dimension 1 Code","Global Dimension 2 Code");
22
23  UpdateReferencedIds;
24  SetLastModifiedDateTime;
25
26  ⊞OnModify()...
```

Since Microsoft Dynamics NAV 2016, Microsoft has evolved the application by introducing **Events**.

**Events** are something like *integration points* inside the Microsoft Dynamics NAV application, and they allow the execution of customized processes (functions) in response to specific actions that occur on the ERP and to separate custom functionalities from the standard application business logic.

Events in Microsoft Dynamics NAV consist of three different elements:

- **Event**: The declaration of the action in the application. This is a C/AL function (event publisher function).
- **Publisher**: The object that contains the event declaration. It exposes an event to the outside world.
- **Subscriber**: The object that listens for and handles a published event raised by the system. This is normally a function that subscribes to a published event and includes the business logic to handle this event.

Events are fired before and after a trigger (for example, when a new record is inserted in a table, the system first raises the OnBeforeInsertEvent event, then the OnInsert trigger, and finally the OnAfterInsertEvent event) or between standard Microsoft's code (Microsoft has added many events to the standard code that you can subscribe to for customizing the standard business processes).

An event can have multiple subscribers. In this case, the execution order of different functions subscribed to the same event is random and may change at any time. When you develop a solution, you need to keep in mind that the business logic needs to be independent of the execution orders in cases such as these.

There are five types of events:

- **Database events**: Automatically raised by the system when it performs database operations on a table object, such as deleting, inserting, modifying, and renaming a record, as defined in a table.
- **Page events**: Raised automatically by the system when it performs certain operations in a page object.
- **Business events**: Custom events that are raised by C/AL code. They define a formal contract that carries an implicit promise not to change in future releases.
- **Integration events**: Custom events that are raised by C/AL code, such as a business event, except that it does not carry the same promise of not changing.
- **Global Events**: Predefined system events that are automatically raised by codeunit 1 (**application management**).

 With NAV (C/AL), always check the **Event Subscription** view (**Tools | Debugger | Event Subscription**) where you can find all the subscribers attached to a published event and if parameters mismatch occurs. AL enforces this parameter check by giving a compilation error.

When implementing an event-based solution with C/AL, you need to do the following:

- Publish the event (create a function that is an event publisher function)
- Raise the event (create the code that calls the event publisher function)
- Subscribe to the event

*Chapter 2*

For example, if you want to create a subscriber function to `OnBeforeInsertEvent` of the `Sales Header` table, you need to define the function as follows:

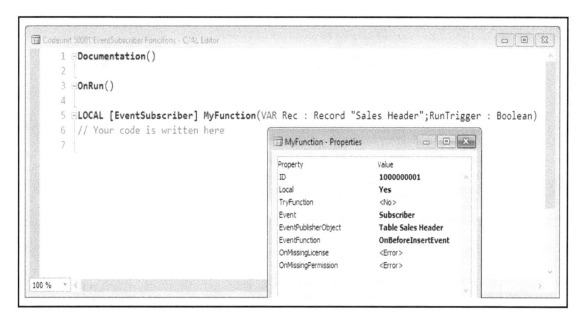

When creating an event subscriber, you need to provide the following parameters:

- `EventPublisherObject`: Is the object that raises the event.
- `EventFunction`: Is the publisher's event that we want to subscribe to. When subscribing to a particular event, the system asks to overwrite the signature of the function, to match the event signature.
- `OnMissingLicense`: Here, we can specify what the system should do if the license in use does not have the permissions to access the subscribed object. The options are as follows:
    - `Error`: An error is thrown and the execution is stopped (default)
    - `Skip`: The event is not executed and no errors are thrown
- `OnMissingPermission`: Here, we can specify what the system should do if the user that executes the event doesn't have the permissions to access the object. The options are as follows:
    - `Error`: An error is thrown and the execution is stopped (default)
    - `Skip`: The event is not executed and no errors are thrown

**[ 35 ]**

If `EventFunction` selected is related to an event triggered by a table field (for example, `OnBeforeValidateEvent`), the system asks for a new property called `EventPublisherElement`. Here, we have to select the table field that triggers the event that we want to subscribe to:

| Property | Value |
| --- | --- |
| **OnAfterValidateCustomer - Properties** | |
| ID | 1101340007 |
| Local | Yes |
| TryFunction | <No> |
| Event | Subscriber |
| EventPublisherObject | Table Customer |
| EventFunction | OnAfterValidateEvent |
| EventPublisherElement | Customer Posting Group |
| OnMissingLicense | <Error> |
| OnMissingPermission | <Error> |

The signature of this `EventSubscriber` will be the following:

```
LOCAL [EventSubscriber] OnAfterValidateCustomer(VAR Rec : Record Customer;VAR xRec : Record Customer;CurrFieldNo : Integer)
```

As you can imagine, events are a powerful way for creating customized codes without affecting the base application. By using events, you can decouple your code from the standard code.

If we consider the previous example, without using events we need to place the `MyFunction` call inside the `OnInsert` trigger of the `Sales Header` table, and this requires modifying a standard object. Instead, by using events, the standard object is not modified and the `MyFunction` code is defined in a new object totally independent from Microsoft code.

By using events, the code becomes easier to maintain and to upgrade. An upgrade of the baseline of the application (standard Microsoft code) will not have an impact on your code, and so the upgrade process will become easier, quicker, and less costly.

Microsoft has done (and it is doing continuously) work on adding events to the standard code base. For example, this is a comparison between the codeunit 80 in NAV 2017 and the same codeunit in NAV 2018:

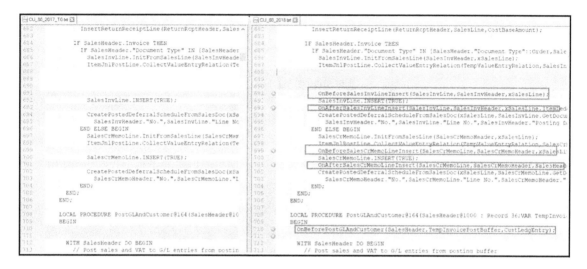

Events added by Microsoft in standard code. Note the number of red boxes on the right.

Red boxes are events that were not present in previous versions of the application. These are all hooks that you can use to customize standard code.

# The new Extensions 2.0 model

Using events in your code is basically of the new way of developing applications for Microsoft Dynamics NAV/Dynamics 365 Business Central and is referred to as extensions.

An **extension** is defined as *"an installable feature of Microsoft Dynamics NAV functionality built in a way that does not directly alter source resources and is distributed as a preconfigured package"*.

The new extension model allows you to create a solution for Microsoft Dynamics NAV or Microsoft Dynamics 365 Business Central that is deployed as a package (.app file).

This package is developed using the new AL language by extending standard objects and using events for creating custom business logic or modifying the existing standard behavior.

We'll consider here only what is called *Extensions 2.0*. The previous model, *Extensions 1.0* introduced in NAV 2016, is now deprecated.

A solution based on extensions can be represented as in the following diagram:

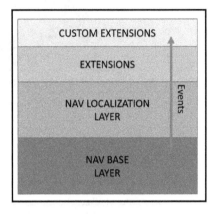

As you can see, in an extension-based solution, all layers are well defined. Integration between layers is managed by using events, and the code is cleaner.

You can have as many extensions as you want in your solutions (just like a *puzzle*), and combining them all together will permit you to have a customized solution that will be easy to upgrade and maintain in the future:

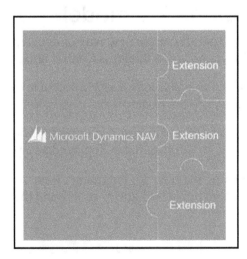

Traditional Microsoft Dynamics NAV objects developed using C/AL language are packaged in a format called **Financial Object** (**FOB**), and by creating a FOB package you can easily move customizations between systems.

The main differences between the old `.fob` package and the new `.app` package are summarized in the following table:

| `.fob` objects | `.app` objects |
| --- | --- |
| Package: financial object, standard old objects package | Package: extensions-based: `.al` files, `app.json`, `launch.json` |
| Source code visible in C/SIDE | NO |
| Includes standard objects and new objects, and standard code can be changed | NO |
|  | Extensions of standard objects plus additional business logic plus new objects. Event-based |
| Imported in NAV database via C/SIDE | Deployed via PowerShell, VS code |

In the new Extension model, customizations are done in Visual Studio Code by using AL language (we'll cover that in more detail in the next chapters), and the solution is file-based (the code is no longer maintained in the database, but placed externally in `.al` files).

Visual Studio Code and the AL Language extension permit you to do the following:

- Create new files for your solution (an extension can be composed of different .al files)
- Get assistance with creating the appropriate configuration and setting files
- Use code snippets that provide templates for coding application objects and create new code snippets to automate tasks
- Get compiler validation and code analysis while coding
- Directly publish your customizations (by pressing *F5*)
- Debug

The following objects are available today with the AL Language extension for Visual Studio Code:

- Table object
- Table Extension object
- Page object
- Page Extension object

- Codeunit object
- Report object
- XmlPort object
- Query object
- Control Add-in (Javascript)
- Profile and Page Customizations

We'll cover each one of these objects in detail in the following chapters.

Extensions packages are installed on a per-tenant basis (a tenant is an instance of Dynamics 365 Business Central running on the Microsoft cloud). When you install an extension into the Dynamics 365 Business Central database (or in NAV 2018), you cannot see the objects and the code exactly like in the classic C/SIDE environment. Now there are different system tables that store all the metadata for an extension:

- **NAV App Object Metadata**: This is a system table that stores the metadata deltas for the extensions.
- **NAV App Tenant App**: It stores all extensions installed on a tenant that are part of the application database. This table is synchronized with the NAV App Installed App table, and it's also used for supporting the *on-the-fly* app switching.
- **NAV App Data Archive**: These are tables created to archive data for uninstalled extensions and it's used restore data when reinstalling or upgrading extensions.
- **NAV App Installed App**: Tt contains information about the extensions installed on a tenant.
- **NAV App**: It contains all published extensions for an application database.
- **NAV App Dependencies**: It contains all the published extension dependencies.
- **NAV App Capabilities**: It contains the list of capabilities for every published extension. This information comes from the extension manifest file.
- **NAV App Object Prerequisites**: It contains the list of prerequisite objects for every published extension.
- **Tenant Permission Set**: It contains all the mappings between the extensions and permission sets.
- **Tenant Permission**: It contains all the permissions for objects as defined in every permission set in the extension packages.

If you have an extension that adds a field to a table (for example, a new field called Customer Category in the Customer table) and check the application database, you will not be able to see the added field. The extension fields on a table are not visible in C/SIDE, but are visible if you run the table.

If you check the database, you will see that now we have a table with the same name as the original table (`Customer`) plus the extension's ID. In this table, you have all the newly added fields from that extension (plus the primary key of the original table):

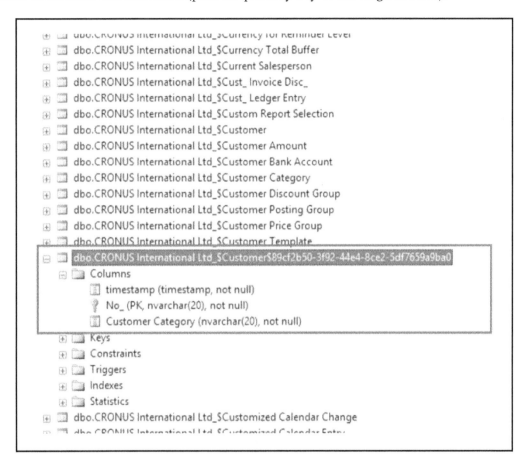

Objects in extensions are free for the customer (no need to pay to add objects), but when developing extensions for Dynamics 365 Business Central, we have a set of rules for the object IDs to respect:

- **50.000-99.999**: This is the range to use for per-tenant or customer customizations (no AppSource).

- **1.000.000-60.000.000**: This is the RSP range for partners that have an ISV solution for Dynamics 365 Business central SaaS or an on-premises one. When used in Business Central, these extensions are obtained as apps from `appsource.microsoft.com`.
- **70.000.000-74.999.999**: This range is only available for extension development and only in Dynamics 365 Business Central (SaaS solution). These extensions are obtained as apps from `appsource.microsoft.com`.

# Running C/SIDE and AL side by side

As previously described, in the new extension model you can develop customizations by using Visual Studio Code and the AL language. However, Microsoft Dynamics NAV 2018 actually supports development using both C/SIDE and AL. In this scenario, when new objects are added or changed in the C/SIDE environment, these changes must be reflected in the symbol download in Visual Studio Code (only in this way the AL language extension is able to provide intelliSense for the objects).

To enable this reflection, a new command argument has been added to `finsql.exe`:

```
finsql.exe Command=generatesymbolreference, Database="Demo Database NAV
(11-0)", ServerName=NAVSRV
```

This command will add symbol references to the `NAV App Object Metadata` table for the specified database.

To have a symbol reference added to the `NAV App Object Metadata` table on every object compilation in C/SIDE, you need to start `finsql.exe` each time with the following argument:

```
finsql.exe generatesymbolreference=yes
```

The default value is `NO`, to *not* generate a symbol reference on every compilation.

At server level, the **Enable loading application symbol reference at server startup** flag must be enabled to allow symbol generation. If the setting is not enabled, the `generatesymbolreference` setting does not have any effect:

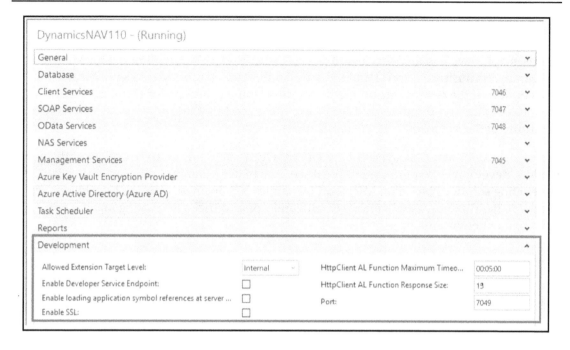

# Scalable and SaaS-ready solutions

Extensions are the basic pattern for implementing SaaS-ready solutions. To be scalable and ready for a SaaS business model, an extension has to meet some requirements:

- It should be a small module with defined functionalities.
- It must be easy to install and upgrade.
- It should have a guided setup (wizard) and setup tables should be pre-populated.
- The setup should be executed without having administrator permissions. If the extension adds new objects to the base application, you need to provide the appropriate permission sets.
- It must support all the possible standard configurations of the base application.
- The user interface must respect specific guidelines.
- The extension must support translations in different languages (**XML Localization Interchange File Format**, or **XLIFF**).
- The extension should raise integration event to other extensions, to be extendable.
- The extension should support different localizations of the base application.

# Summary

In this chapter, we had an overview of the event-based development model for Microsoft Dynamics 365 Business Central and the benefits that it offers for developers. We also had an overview of the new extension model for developing solutions for Dynamics 365 Business Central (on-premises and SaaS) and the impact that this new model will have on the future of the Microsoft ERP customizations.

In `Chapter 3`, *Modern Development Environment Overview*, we'll see an overview of the new modern development environment. We'll see how to use Visual Studio Code for developing solutions based on Microsoft Dynamics 365 Business Central, how to customize it, how to handle source-code management, and tips and tricks for having an efficient development environment.

# 3
# Modern Development Environment Overview

In `Chapter 2`, *The New Extension Model*, we introduced what extending an application means and we tasted the new extensibility model for Microsoft Dynamics 365 Business Central.

In this chapter, we will provide you with an overview of the new Microsoft Dynamics 365 Business Central modern development environment and we will help you to configure its core application, Visual Studio Code, for developing extensions and solutions targeted for a single tenant or SaaSified for AppSource. SaaSify is a neologism typically used by Microsoft Dynamics NAV developers when moving standard legacy C/AL customization to certified cloud-ready AL solutions for Microsoft Dynamics 365 Business Central.

We will also learn how to use and create customized AL snippets to squeeze the maximum out of an efficient development environment.

By the end of the chapter, we will have also learned **source-code management** (**SCM**) with the powerful Visual Studio Code Git native integration.

This chapter will cover the following:

- What the components of the new modern development environment are, compared with a classic CSIDE development environment
- What the AL language is
- How to create and use AL snippets to be more productive
- Visual Studio Code installation, setup, and configuration to develop extensions targeted for Microsoft Dynamics 365 Business Central
- A basic introduction to Microsoft Dynamics 365 Business Central SCM using Git

# Modern versus classic development environments

The history and success of Microsoft Dynamics 365 Business Central's predecessor, Microsoft Dynamics NAV, starts with classic client.

From day one, this Visual C++ application was promising and after some decades of glory its retirement looks quite near. It will be replaced by the more modern, shiny, multi-platform, web application development-oriented Visual Studio Code.

Classic client used to be a two-sided application: a first-in-class production client for end users and at the same time a suitable workbench for developers.

With Microsoft Dynamics NAV 2013, it was deprecated as a production client and just simply named **CSIDE (Client server integrated development environment)**, relegated to only a development application targeted as a Windows and/or web client.

# Characteristics and advantages of CSIDE

CSIDE comes with native support for a proprietary language called **C/AL** (**Client/Application Language**), a solid and robust development language engineered to customize or build horizontal and vertical solutions for ERP applications. Both the platform (CSIDE) and the language (C/AL) have evolved and been enriched with features and functions, major release after major release, reflecting the focus and great investment that Microsoft dedicates to its top SMB ERP product in the Microsoft Dynamics family.

Within CSIDE and Microsoft Dynamics NAV, as typically happens in many competitor on-premises ERP applications, it is still possible to customize, up to completely changing, the standard core application code provided. This quite big advantage comes with the disadvantage of maintaining these customizations or solutions over the years. This typically leads to making the upgrade process to higher versions a time consuming and costly procedure that most of the time delays the evolution of the ERP implementation and its infrastructure.

Together with the capability of changing the standard application, there are a few other advantages offered by CSIDE. The main ones are listed here:

- Provides a graphical interface to easily represent and edit object metadata. To give an example, by pressing *Shift + F4* or by pressing the **Properties** button within CSIDE, you can directly inspect the property of the selected object (table, field, code unit, page, column, and so on) in a card format.
- Export and import compressed portable binary objects (proprietary `.fob` format). FOB files are lightweight, easy to handle, and source protected (binary) files that permit the source code to be stored directly inside the database and serialized in and deserialized out through CSIDE.
- Work easily with thousands of objects. The famous Object Designer (*Shift + F12* from the CSIDE development environment) is the all-in-one mature development tool that over several decades has been enriched with many features, such as managing translation files, setting breakpoints, running the debugger, synchronizing metadata changes, running data upgrades, and many more. But the top capability is still its tabular Excel-like list representation of objects and advanced filtering, which makes the developer's life easier and more productive, even in the most complex scenario, when developing vertical solutions against thousands of application objects (new or changed).
- Symbol references and metadata structure changes are automatically generated or modified right after compilation.

When compiling an object (*F11* from Object Designer), choosing the option to synchronize the metadata changes now, stored as `BLOB` fields in the `Object Metadata` table, are automatically updated and developers can benefit from this by having an always up to date intelliSense feature. In simple words, object metadata changes and symbol updates are tightly coupled and consistently in sync.

There might be many more advantages that can be added to that feature list, but the ones reported are the most common, in comparison with a Visual Studio Code based development environment.

# Characteristics and advantages of Visual Studio Code

It is important to understand at this point that such differences come mainly because of different development targets and the ERP deployment model they are streamlined for. CSIDE is optimized for on-premises, while Visual Studio Code was born to rule web-based cloud application development, and it is the only one that can and should be used to extend the Microsoft Dynamics 365 Business Central application.

Visual Studio Code is worldwide most used light-weight, multi-platform editor and can be for free from: `https://code.visualstudio.com/`.

Its strength and success are mainly due to open source extensibility through its built-in API. This leads to a richness in languages and runtimes (C#, Python, C/C++, PowerShell and so on.) and a huge, long list of development utilities (`.NET` based, project handling, refactoring, containers, Azure routines, and so on).

Other characteristics of Visual Studio Code can be resumed here:

- **Code centric**: As per its name and nature, it is all about coding and making things fast, simple, and productive. There are no **graphical user interfaces** (**GUIs**) to display object metadata as there are in the CSIDE development environment.

- **Folder based**: Compared to, for example, Visual Studio, this is not project-based, but it simply deals with files and folders. Many of the extension utilities that are currently in the Visual Studio Code online marketplace provide enhancement of file and directory handling, `.txt` or `.xml` or `.json` editing, revisioning, text highlights, and so on.

- **Native integration with version control** (**Git**): Compared to CSIDE, this is a huge advancement, since the old development environment did not come with an out-of-the-box SCM system. If you have been in the Microsoft Dynamics NAV business for a while as a partner or an **independent software vendor** (**ISV**), you might have discovered how hard is to keep all the code changes and versioning in sync when you have many developers working on the same application base.

# Anatomy of Visual Studio Code workspace

The workspace interface is made of different areas, as shown in the following screenshot:

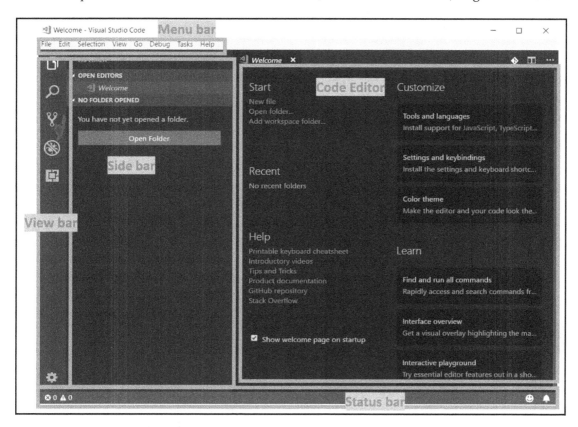

These are described in the following sections.

# Menu bar

Menu Bar of Visual Studio Code

As a best-in-class code editor made by developers for developers, Visual Studio Code provides a number of shortcuts that make editing faster. If you are new to Visual Studio Code, you might want to inspect the **Menu** bar for a list of shortcuts or **Help | Keyboard Shortcuts References** to download a PDF file for the full list. I would encourage you to print this on paper and place it in front of you as a daily reminder.

## View bar

This is just a shortcut to enable the context for different sidebar, depending on the type of development activity you are looking for:

To open, edit, or inspect files and folders, use this:

 **Explorer** (*Ctrl + Shift + E*).

This enables advanced search capabilities (even regular expressions) inside the file or folders currently open as workspaces in the explorer bar. It should offer, in the end, the same experience as CSIDE, but in a different output format, since there is no Excel tabular concept with Visual Studio Code:

 **Search** (*Ctrl + Shift + F*)

Visual Studio Code natively supports Git source control management and it is tightly bound to it. Right after the installation, you will be prompted several times to download and install Git, if not already done, on your local machine. Git installation on Windows is straightforward and you might become experienced at using it. There are many ways to download and install it:

 **Source Control** (*Ctrl + Shift + G*)

The latest official build is available for download on the Git website. Just go to `http://git-scm.com/download/win` and the download will start automatically.

 **Debug** (*Ctrl + Shift + D*)

The debugger in Visual Studio Code is natively supported only for Node.js. We will see in a later chapter that Microsoft Dynamics 365 Business Central Debugger can be invoked after the installation of the AL language extension, and its outputs will be displayed in this area.

 **Extensions** (*Ctrl* + *Shift* + *X*)

Displays and manages Visual Studio Code extensions downloaded on demand from the online marketplace or installed manually as VSIX files.

# Sidebar

Depending on where you navigate from the view bar, this enables different context-sensitive sidebar: Explorer, Search, Source Control, Debug, and Extensions. Other views and relative sidebar can be added through different open source extensions downloadable from the online marketplace (for example, Docker, Microsoft Azure, and so on).

# Code editor

This is where developers will spend most of their time; it is the file editing area. Therefore, it takes most of the space of the application. But if this is not enough for you to concentrate on your current coding, when you have a file highlighted, just try pressing *Ctrl* + *K Z*, and you enter **Zen** mode where the application goes into full-screen mode and your file is aligned and sitting right in front of you in all its beauty.

# Status bar

The status bar displays information about the currently selected file or folder, as shown here:

Status bar in action

 For example, from the screenshot, you can see that an AL file is selected from the ALProject6 folder; it contains two errors and the cursor is placed exactly at line 12, column 12.

# Tips to work efficiently in Visual Studio Code

Visual Studio Code is a continuously evolving development editor and the best tips that we can provide to start working with proficiency with it are these features:

- Go to **Help | Interactive Playground** and try out all the great features that come with it out of the box, and familiarize yourself with the one you think might be most useful in your daily development work. This screenshot shows a list of these:

> - Multi-cursor Editing - block selection, select all occurrences, add additional cursors and more
> - IntelliSense - get code assistance and parameter suggestions for your code and external modules.
> - Line Actions - quickly move lines around to re-order your code.
> - Rename Refactoring - quickly rename symbols across your code base.
> - Refactoring via Extraction - quickly extract common code into a separate function or constant.
> - Formatting - keep your code looking great with inbuilt document & selection formatting.
> - Code Folding - focus on the most relevant parts of your code by folding other areas.
> - Errors and Warnings - see errors and warning as you type.
> - Snippets - spend less time typing with snippets.

- Memorize and get used to tips and tricks provided by the Visual Studio Code community worldwide. You can start with the most commonly reported ones here: `https://code.visualstudio.com/docs/getstarted/tips-and-tricks#vscode`.
- Get your hands dirty every time there is an update or a new release of Visual Studio Code. Click on **Help | Release Notes** and play with all the ones listed that you might think will be helpful for your job.

# The AL Extension

Visual Studio Code can be considered just a simple and powerful code editor as is.

What gives this application its sixth gear and credentials as a real modern development environment is the AL Extension created and engineered by the Microsoft Dynamics 365 Business Central Development Team.

The AL Extension is Built using the standard Visual Studio Code API; it can be deployed in the following ways:

- **Directly** as a downloadable package from the Visual Studio Code marketplace. Targeted only for Microsoft Dynamics 365 Business Central.
- **Manually** as an installable package (VSIX) from the product DVD. Targeted only for on- premises Microsoft Dynamics NAV.

Even if they might look like the same, they are consistently different, since VSIX is coming from the on-premises product DVD and is currently just a cut-off, limited version from the fall of 2017 and does not contain all the enhancements and new features made by the modern development team up to now. These features will be exclusively reserved for the Microsoft Dynamics 365 Business Central cloud-based development until the next major on-premises version.

The old legacy CSIDE development environment was based on the C/AL language. Its successor is very similar in its coding statement, but, being streamlined for cloud development, it is not designed to change the standard code but to greatly extend it. That is what AL language was made for.

# Comparison of capabilities supported by CSIDE and Visual Studio Code

The following is a comparison matrix of capabilities supported by CSIDE (C/AL) and/or Visual Studio Code (AL):

| Object Type | C/AL | AL |
| --- | --- | --- |
| Page | YES | YES |
| Page Extension | | YES |
| Table | YES | YES |
| Table Extension | | YES |
| Codeunit | YES | YES |
| Report | YES | YES |
| Xmlport | YES | YES |
| Query | YES | YES |
| Menu Suite | YES | Replacement |
| Permission Set | YES | YES |

| Web Service | YES | YES |
|---|---|---|
| Table Data | YES | YES |
| Custom Report Layout | YES | YES |
| Translation | YES | YES |
| .NET Interoperability Reference | YES | Only for on-premise in Fall 2018 Update |
| Control Add-In | YES | YES |

# Getting started with AL language

To start with AL language, simply download it from the marketplace by following these simple steps:

1. Run Visual Studio Code
2. Click on the **Extensions** view bar
3. In the search field, type `Microsoft Dynamics 365 Business Central`
4. Click on **Install** and when you have finished installing, reload Visual Studio Code as requested:

AL Language extension

At the time we are writing, the AL Language Extension has been downloaded 18,290 times (shown by the **18K** notation, top right); this is a huge number for a product that was released just a few months ago, compared to the decennial CSIDE community. It's also worth mentioning that the build number is **0.15**. The 15th major version of the AL language is compatible only with Microsoft Dynamics 365 Business Central. This version is not supported for creating extensions with Microsoft Dynamics NAV, which has its own VSIX file dispatched with the product DVD and has a build number of **0.12**.

Once the AL Language is installed and enabled in Visual Studio Code, you can start to develop your own extension from scratch.

As step 1, invoke the Command Palette (*Ctrl + Shift + P*) and select **AL:GO**! or use the simple shortcut Alt + *A, Alt + L*.

If you are not familiar, still, with the Visual Studio Code keyboard shortcuts, Command Palette will give you access to a vast plethora of the functionality for the most common operations.

# Developing your first extension with AL language

AL language will be activated and prompt you to provide the path for an empty folder. This will be the folder where we will develop our first extension.

Type `C:\APPREPO\MYFIRSTEXT` (this is just a fantasy folder name) and hit return. You'll be presented with 2 development choices:

- **Microsoft Cloud sandbox**: This is the choice to go with when you have already subscribed for a trial or paid version for Microsoft Dynamics 365 Business Central. We are assuming that you have already created your own trial or paid version so that this is the option you have to choose at this stage. Bear in mind that connection will only be done in a sandbox environment and never to the production environment. Direct development in production tenants is, of course, not supported.
- **Your own server**: This is reserved for Docker-contained deployment in a local machine or Azure VMs (or an on-premises Microsoft Dynamics NAV Server connection). We will inspect these deployment options in a later chapter.

Since we choose to develop against our own Microsoft Dynamics 365 Business Central sandbox, a new modal authentication window will open requesting credentials (login and password) to connect to the sandbox.

Please note that credentials are stored within the Visual Studio Code session. If you need to connect to another sandbox tenant or simply want to reset them, just invoke the command palette (*Ctrl + Shift + P*) and select **AL:Clear credentials cache**.

That's all.

What happened here is we simply store the credentials to connect to the sandbox and a basic `hello world` example in the AL Language structure has been created on the fly in the specified folder.

The simplest initial structure for an AL Extension is made of:

`.vscode` subfolder containing `launch.json` file:

The `launch.json` file configures the connection and interaction between Visual Studio Code and the external sandbox environment or, for On Premises, the Microsoft Dynamics NAV Server.

The interaction is bidirectional and the main purposes are these:

- Pull out through NAV Server requests the symbols stored in the tenant database.
- Push (publish), install and synchronize the extension created inside the tenant database.

```json
1  {
2      "version": "0.2.0",
3      "configurations": [
4          {
5              "type": "al",
6              "request": "launch",
7              "name": "Microsoft cloud sandbox",
8              "startupObjectId": 22,
9              "startupObjectType": "Page"
10         }
11     ]
12 }
```

Typical for on-premises installation is to change the option to connect to Microsoft Dynamics NAV Server service. You can check which are the available options by pressing *Ctrl + space* inside the `launch.json` file. For more information visit: `https://docs.microsoft.com/en-us/dynamics365/business-central/dev-itpro/developer/devenv-json-files`

`app.json` file:

It is a manifest file in json notation and it is used to declare specific properties of the extensions that will be parsed when publishing or installing the app.

Extension or app terms are used quite often as synonymous by AL developers.

Here is a sample screenshot:

```json
1  {
2      "id": "b4a07b21-6615-45ef-8511-13e9c39ab01f",
3      "name": "MyFirstExtension",
4      "publisher": "Default publisher",
5      "brief": "This is a brief description of my extension",
6      "description": "This is a more detailed and verbose description",
7      "version": "1.0.0.0",
8      "privacyStatement": "https://privacy.microsoft.com/en-us/privacystatement",
9      "EULA": "https://privacy.microsoft.com/en-us/EULA",
10     "help": "https://bc.dtacconi.com/en-us/Help",
11     "url": "https://bc.dtacconi.com/en-us/ExtensionDescription",
12     "logo": "C:\\TEMP\\MyFirstExt.bmp",
13     "capabilities": [],
14     "dependencies": [],
15     "screenshots": [],
16     "platform": "12.0.0.0",
17     "application": "12.0.0.0",
18     "idRange": {
19         "from": 50100,
20         "to": 50149
21     }
22  }
```

Json notation used to declare specific properties of the extensions in the app.json file

Here are a few elements from the preceding screenshot:

- **ID** is automatically generated for you when you create a new project. Changing the ID will cause the platform to view this as a completely different extension.
- If the extension depends on one or more extensions, the ID, name and publisher of the extension, at least, must be specified in the `dependencies` Json array.
- The `application` and `platform` version must match the symbols that will be or have been downloaded. They should also match the destination tenant when publishing/installing.

To know more about the Json files, please visit this link: `https://docs.microsoft.com/en-us/dynamics365/business-central/dev-itpro/developer/devenv-json-files`.

# HelloWorld.al sample

This is the classic `hello world` sample, created automatically.

What enables and activates the AL language code parser and intellisense is simply the `.al` file extension `.al`. You might notice that the file extension is shown in the status bar, at the bottom right. There are several development file and folder best practices and naming conventions for AL objects, to better and more productively handle these in complex extension or vertical solution. If the extension targets the marketplace (AppSource), then the naming convention has restrictive rules that must be strictly applied. A taste of these best practice can be found here: `https://docs.microsoft.com/en-us/dynamics365/business-central/dev-itpro/compliance/apptest-bestpracticesforalcode`.

Once the AL Extension structure is in place, it needs to have suitable symbols to activate intellisense and object references. To make a comparison with CSIDE and C/AL, this can be resumed as the entire set of object definition whom you compile against. This is needed to validate the definition of your extension and the environment that this has to work and interact with. To download symbols, just run the Command Palette (*Ctrl + Shift + P*) and click on **AL:Download symbols**. This will instruct AL Language to perform an HTTP request to your sandbox development endpoint presenting the credentials stored initially to pull out the symbols. At the same time, a new subfolder will be created, named `.alpackages`, to store the symbols. In this simple example, there are two symbols:

- `Microsoft_Application_12.x.xxxxx.x.app`
- `Microsoft_System_12.0.xxxxx.x.app`

The system symbol app contains all the definitions and references for system and virtual tables. The application symbol app contains all the other object definition and references (tables, pages, reports, code units, and so on).

Just in case your development requires dependency on other extensions, defined in the `app.json` file, symbols for these required extensions are also downloaded at this stage.

 Try to go in the `.alpackages` folder, rename the files `.app` into `.zip`, and extract their content. You will then have better clear in details how a symbol app is made of.

When there are no symbols downloaded, typically .al files are highlighted in red, since there is nothing to validate their references inside. Exactly right after all the symbols are downloaded, the AL Extension applies a check of all .al files against them and if there are no references or syntax errors, .al file color in the sidebar changes from red to the normal font theme color.

Now everything is in place to build the extension package and publish it against the sandbox.

To build the extension package, run the Command Palette (*Ctrl* +*Shift* + *B*) and click on **AL:Package** (*Ctrl* +*Shift* + *P*). If no error arises, the package builds successfully and a file with the syntax `<publisher>_<name>_<version>.app` should have been created in the main folder.

> Try to go to the main folder, rename the .app into .zip, and extract its content. You will have better clear in details how an extension/app is assembled and packaged.

Running the Command Palette (*Ctrl* +*Shift* + *B*) and clicking **AL:Publish** (*F5*) will produce a push of the extension into the sandbox tenant and a subsequent run of the web client that connects to the tenant, to verify the effectiveness of the changes made.

# AL snippets

Code snippets are pieces or small template of codes that can be recycled and reused through the intellisense feature for fast application coding. These are typically used to rapidly create

- Object structure definition (for example, a table, field, page, report, xmlport, and so on)
- Looping statements (for example, for, repeat until, while, and so on)

AL Snippets come with the prefix *t*, followed by a meaningful name. To show them up, go to the `HelloWorld.al`, hit return at the end of `Message(...)`, and type `t`. Intellisense will show up a list for the current standard code snippets dispatched with AL Extension for Microsoft Dynamics 365 Business Central.

You can practice yourself by choosing some of them and populating the relevant placeholders to create a meaningful script.

You can see from this table a list of the standard snippets. This standard list can be extended in future updates and enhanced for AL Extension:

| Metadata Structure | Statement Brick | Field | Object |
|---|---|---|---|
| taction | tassert | tfield | tcodeunit |
| tcaptionml | tcaseelse | tfieldcode | tcontroladdin |
| teventbus | tcaseof | tfieldoption | tpage (card) |
| teventint | tfor | tfieldtext | tpage (list) |
| teventsub | tforeach | | tpagecust |
| tkey | tif | | tpageext |
| toptioncaptionml | tifelse | | tprofile |
| tpagefield | tisempty | | tquery |
| tprocedure | tisemptyelse | | treport |
| ttrigger | trepeat | | ttable |
| tusercontrol | twhile | | ttableext |
| | twithdo | | txmlport |

Aside from the standard snippets, we are able to create our own snippets. To accomplish this easy task, choose these options: Go to **File** | **Preferences** | **User Snippets**

You can also choose these options: Run Command Palette (*Ctrl + Shift + P*) and select **Preferences: Configure user snippets**.

Choose Al.json (AL). This is the file where you have to store your own code snippet and its comment already provides good hints on how to operate it:

```
{
// Place your snippets for al here. Each snippet is defined under a snippet
name and has a prefix, body and
// description. The prefix is what is used to trigger the snippet and the
body will be expanded and inserted. Possible variables are:
// $1, $2 for tab stops, $0 for the final cursor position, and ${1:label},
${2:another} for placeholders. Placeholders with the
// same ids are connected.
// Example:
// "Print to console": {
//   "prefix": "log",
//   "body": [
//       "console.log('$1');",
//       "$2
//   ],
//   "description": "Log output to console"
// }
```

The CSIDE development environment does not offer anything similar to the Visual Studio Code AL Snippet feature.

# Creating our own snippets

To demonstrate how easy and powerful it is to work with snippets, let's start by creating our own.

1. The following code snippet will add to the application a `message` statement, changing the `Al.json` file as shown here:

```
"Message": {
    "prefix": "tMessage",
    "body": [
        "MESSAGE('[' + FORMAT($1) + ']:$1');",
        "$2"
    ],
    "description": "Display the field or variable selected"
}
```

2. Go back to `HelloWorld.al` file and change the page extension signature to use a different ID and extend `Customer Card`:

```
0 references
pageextension 50149 CustomerCardExt extends "Customer Card"
{
    trigger OnOpenPage();
    begin
        Message('App published: Hello world');
    end;
}
```

3. At the end of the message statement line, hit *Return* and in the new line press *t*. This will activate intellisense and show you a series of snippets.

4. Choose `tMessage`, and it will automatically add the message line with the cursor position ready to accept the name of the field we want to add to the displayed message. Type `Name` and press *tab*.

5. The cursor will complete the line and move to the next one at the speed of light. Type again the letter `t` and select `tMessage`. Type `Address` and press *tab*.

6. In the new line, again press `t` and type `date` and press *Ctrl + space*. Intellisense will recognize that you probably would like to fill in the `FORMAT` statement with a field, and it gives you a different option, choose `Last Date Modified` and press tab.

7. In the end, you will have an extension that will throw you some informational messages from the `Customer Card`:

```
0 references
pageextension 50149 CustomerCardExt extends "Customer Card"
{
    trigger OnOpenPage();
    begin
        Message('App published: Hello world');
        MESSAGE('[' + FORMAT(Name) + ']:Name');
        MESSAGE('[' + FORMAT(Address) + ']:Address');
        MESSAGE('[' + FORMAT("Last Date Modified") + ']:"Last Date Modified"');
    end;
}
```

Create the package (*Ctrl + Shift + B*), publish and install it (*F5*) on to your Microsoft Dynamics 365 Business Central sandbox and have fun in choosing the `Customer Card`.

# Native AL source-code management with Git

The **Source-Code Management** (SCM) is a problem that is amplified coming from a single object created and maintained by a single person for up to several objects (also called a *project* or, with more complexity, *solution*) developed by several persons (also known as teams).

As developers, document and tracking changes is a must, as well as maintaining a chronological history of these changes, the people who performed these changes, and the business reason that lies behind these changes.

Looking at the CSIDE Development Environment, this really has zero footprint out of the box and no documentation related to source-code management. If you browse through official literature or blogs, you might find out how hard it is to maintain a vertical solution with on-premises Microsoft Dynamics NAV in terms of version control, using CSIDE. You might find out partners or customers who blogged about using the Microsoft Visual Studio Team Foundation to track changes in a complex process of extracting an object in text format from CSIDE and then comparing it to PowerShell tools, committing the changes, importing them back with CSIDE... In technical words: a hell of a job.

# Visual Studio Code support to Git

Visual Studio Code is born natively with an open arms support to Git.

What is that? and why Git?

The fun name comes from Linus Torvalds (who is known worldwide as being the inventor and father of Linux OS), which more-or-less means an *unpleasant person* in British English slang. Linus himself described the tool as a "stupid content tracker" but despite this folkloristic story, Git's success has been enormous, and it is currently used worldwide by hundreds of thousands of developers.

Git is an open source version control application engineered to provide a platform for multi-development distributed team work.

It is geared up with several capabilities for the following:

- **Tracking** changes in code
- **Comparing** modifications in code
- **Merging** changes between different application versions

Git and Visual Studio Code are the perfect matching couple, since the latter is fundamentally files and folder based, hence native object comparison and merge have been easily implemented.

Git core is fundamentally based on simple functions executed through a command-line tool, and it does not come natively with any graphical user experience (there is no GUI).

Visual Studio Code, through the Command Palette, is able to interact directly with the common Git functions and commands. The source-code management can then be performed directly without the need for running whatever other fancy tool outside Visual Studio Code interface. You can install Git from `https://git-scm.com/`

Once installed, open Visual Studio Code, and you may notice that in the **SOURCE CONTROL** (*Ctrl + Shift + G*) sidebar there is an action button to initialize repository with the Git icon:

Source Control

Click on the Git icon and select the main folder for the `HelloWorld` extension sample. Push the Initialize Repository button or run Command Palette (*Ctrl + Shift + P*) and then select **Git:Initialize Repository**:

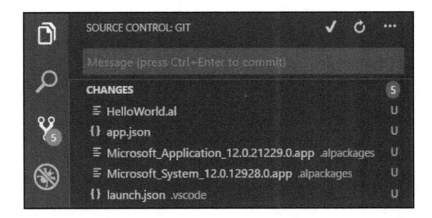

Git:Initialize Repository

Visual Studio Code will detect that you have five files with untracked changes (green **U**). To finalize the repository, you now need to confirm (commit) these files to build the original application baseline.

There are several way to perform this action:

- Run Command Palette (*Ctrl + Shift + P*) and type/select **Git: Stage all changes**
- Click on the **more** action in the **SOURCE CONTROL** activity bar and choose **Stage all changes**.

Code changes in the object are now confirmed to be in stage for the final commit (staged changes) to be integrated into the application base:

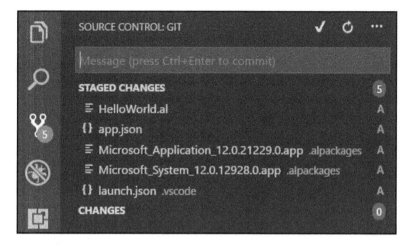

Git: Staging all changes

This is the typical phase where testers kick in for a complete review of the code and runtime checks. If tests pass by successfully, then code can be submitted successfully.

To finalize code changes and commit them, you can try either of these options:

- Run Command Palette (*Ctrl + Shift + P*) and type/select **Git: Commit All**
- Click on the **more** action in the **SOURCE CONTROL** activity bar and choose **Commit All**

Visual Studio Code will prompt you to provide a suitable commit message that should be able to describe the changes applied. You might add your own initial developer number with a task project name or task number, or whatever you think would be understandable in the logs. In this case just type `BC-FirstApp-0001`.

When you hit return, all changes are gone, and you have initialized your baseline application:

Git bar status when all changes are commited

From now on, you can see that all changes are tracked and you can compare, put in stage or discard new changes at will.

This simple example deals with just a local change, but you can expand your knowledge by implementing and orchestrating local changes with global synchronization with remote repositories using GitHub: a brand new product acquisition in the Microsoft family since 2018.

It's in your hands now to decide how you would like to maintain your source code and how deep and complex you want to implement it in your company and/or daily development activity.

# Summary

This chapter has shown you how to set up Visual Studio Code as a modern development environment for Microsoft Dynamics 365 Business Central and how to get started developing your very first extension with AL.

You learned how to work with code snippets, to improve development productivity.

The chapter also gave you a brief introduction to source-code management with Git.

Now you know all you need to know to use Visual Studio Code to develop custom applications. In Chapter 4, *Creating Your Development Sandbox*, we'll see how to use all these concepts to create a more complex extension.

# 4
# Creating Your Development Sandbox

In Chapter 3, *Modern Development Environment Overview*, we gave you an overview of the new modern development environment based on Visual Studio Code for developing extensions for Microsoft Dynamics 365 Business Central, and you had a lot of tips and tricks for customizing and optimizing your development experience.

In this chapter, we'll see how to create an environment isolated from the production one (called a *sandbox*) for developing and testing purposes. Here, we'll learn the following:

- What is a sandbox environment in Dynamics 365 Business Central?
- What are the available types of sandbox environments?
- How to create and use a sandbox environment for testing and developing with Microsoft Dynamics 365 Business Central.

## What is a sandbox?

In Dynamics 365 Business Central, a *sandbox* is an environment totally isolated from a production instance, where you can develop, test, run demos, and play with the service, without affecting the real production data.

You can create a sandbox environment by connecting to your Business Central instance, clicking on the search button in the top bar, and searching for the word *sandbox* (or, if you prefer, by accessing the **Administrator** I **IT Administration** I **General** menu in Dynamics 365 Business Central):

Searching for sandbox in Dynamics 265 Business Central

You will be presented with two main choices:

- Creating an online sandbox
- Creating a container-based sandbox

These are the differences between the two choices:

| Online Sandbox | Container-Based Sandbox |
|---|---|
| Dynamics 365 Cloud Service | Run in Azure VM or locally |
| Managed by Microsoft | Managed by partner |
| Same environment as production | Container-based environment |
| Visual Studio Code only | Visual Studio Code. Supports also C/SIDE and SQL Management Studio |
| Production data manually uploaded using configuration packages | Production data manually uploaded using configuration packages |
| Costs are part of the Business Central subscription | Free if locally-hosted. Azure costs if hosted on Azure VM |

| No database access | Database access available |
|---|---|
| Debugging available | Debugging available |

In the following sections, we'll see how to create a Dynamics 365 Business Central sandbox based on each of these different types.

# Online sandbox

The online sandbox is an environment deployed as a Dynamics 365 Business Central service (SaaS). You can activate the online sandbox only from a production environment, by selecting **Sandbox** in the search box and clicking on the first choice (Sandbox Environment).

When the creation wizard starts, click **Create**:

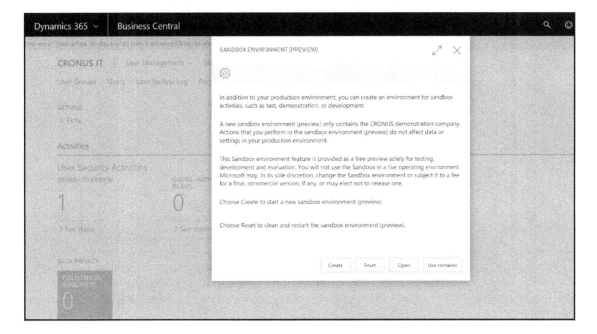

A new browser window will open, and the sandbox creation process starts. At the end of this process, you have a welcome page that shows that the sandbox environment is ready. To start working with the online sandbox, click on the **Close** button:

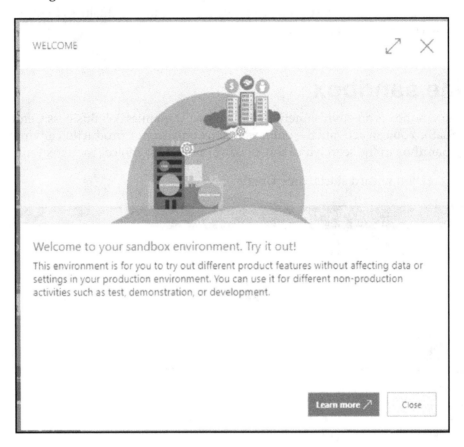

When creating the online sandbox, a new Dynamics 365 Business Central tenant is deployed, and this tenant is created with a default demonstration company (CRONUS). At the moment, there isn't an option for copying data from the production tenant to the online sandbox.

You can reset your online sandbox environment at any time. Remember that resetting the sandbox will completely remove and recreate it with demonstration data. You can switch from the production environment to the sandbox, and you can also limit (via permission sets) the access to the online sandbox for some users.

In the online sandbox, you can create new companies and activate the advanced user experience for Dynamics 365 Business Central. In this environment, you have the in-client designer, and you can develop and debug extensions for Dynamics 365 Business Central, by using Visual Studio Code (and selecting the **Microsoft Cloud Sandbox** option when launching a new AL project with AL:Go!):

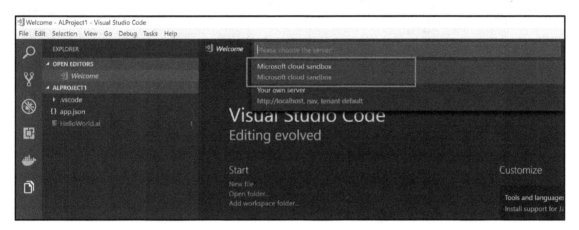

When selecting the Microsoft Cloud sandbox, the launch.json file of your extension project will be as follows:

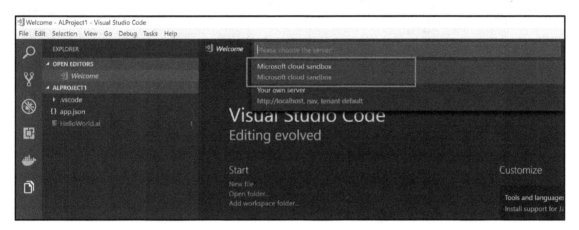

When you download symbols, a request to connect to your Microsoft account will be presented:

# Azure-hosted sandbox

With the Azure-hosted sandbox option, you can create a Dynamics 365 Business Central sandbox on an Azure Virtual Machine, by using a predefined template. This template gives you the option to create an Azure VM with Docker as the infrastructure for the container-based application is automatically configured. Obviously, this option requires that you have an active Azure subscription, and each sandbox has its costs in terms of Azure resources.

To create an Azure-hosted Dynamics 365 Business Central sandbox, select the **Sandbox Environment (Container)** option as shown and then select **Host in Azure**:

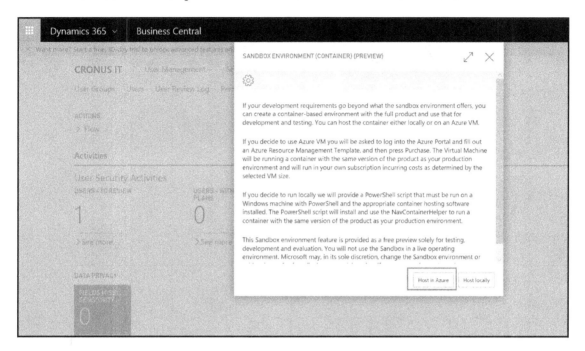

After clicking this button, you will be redirected to your Azure portal account, and the template for the Azure Virtual Machine will be provided:

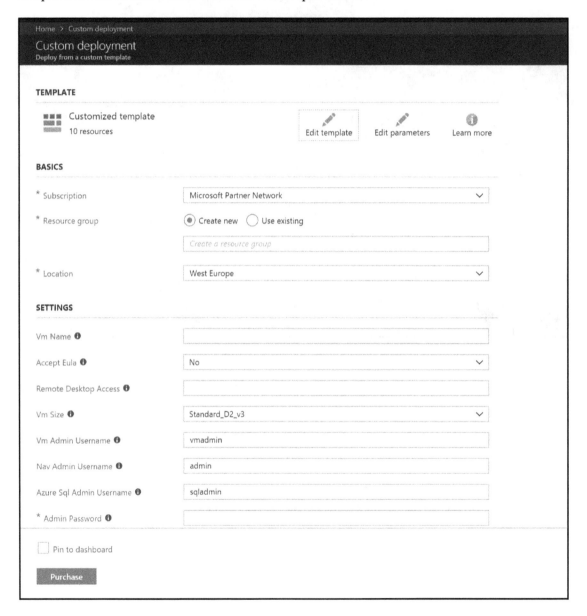

In this template, you with need to select a **Resource group** (or create a new one), select the VM name and the VM admin password (used also for connecting to the Docker-based instance of Dynamics 365 Business Central), select **Accept Eula** is equal to Yes. All the other options are not mandatory.

The VM provides you the correct Docker image version, according to your Dynamics 365 Business Central production tenant:

By clicking on the **Purchase** button, the Azure VM will be automatically provisioned. When the VM is ready for connection, you can immediately start working with Dynamics 365 Business Central and Visual Studio Code. You also have access to C/SIDE.

# Local-hosted sandbox

A local-hosted Dynamics 365 Business Central sandbox requires that you have a machine running Windows 10 or Windows Server 2016, with Docker installed and running.

Docker for Windows can be installed from the following link: `https://www.docker.com/docker-windows`.

Run the installer with administrator privileges. After installation, check that Docker is running Windows Container (right click on the Docker icon in the task bar):

On your Windows **Settings**, check that you've enabled the PowerShell execution script option:

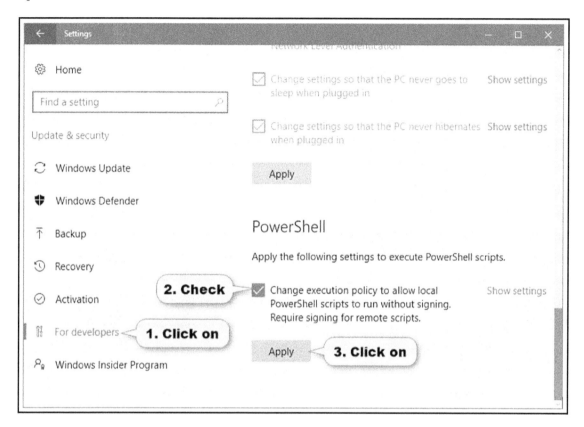

A local-hosted sandbox can be created by selecting the **Sandbox Environment (Container)** option as shown and then selecting **Host locally**:

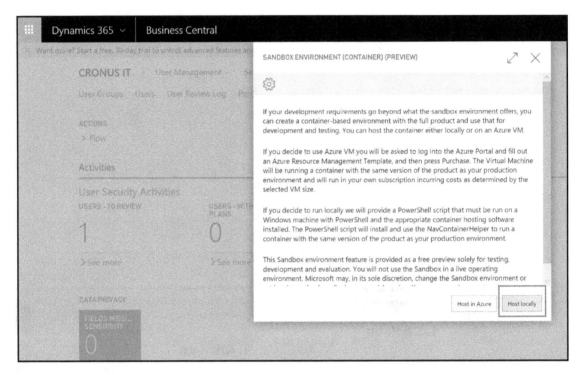

At this point, you will be asked to download and save a Powershell script file called CreateBCSandbox.ps1.

After saving it, start Powershell ISE with administrator privileges and open that file.

In this Powershell script, you've simply to set these parameters:

- Set the $containername variable to the name of your Dynamics 365 Business Central container sandbox.
- Set the $accept_eula variable to '$true':

```
 Amministratore: Windows PowerShell ISE
File  Modifica  Visualizza  Strumenti  Debug  Componenti aggiuntivi  ?

CreateBCSandbox.ps1* X
  1  install-module navcontainerhelper -force
  2
  3  # set accept_eula to $true to accept the eula found here: https://go.microsoft.com/fwlink/?linkid=861843
  4  $accept_eula = $true
  5
  6  $containername = 'D365BC'
  7  $navdockerimage = 'microsoft/bcsandbox:12.0.21229.0'
  8  $appbacpacuri = ''
  9  $tenantbacpacuri = ''
 10
 11  $additionalParameters = @()
 12  if ($appbacpacuri -ne '' -and $tenantbacpacuri -ne '') {
 13      $additionalParameters = @("--env appbacpac="""$appbacpacuri""","--env tenantBacpac="""$tenantbacpacuri""")
 14  }
 15
 16  $credential = get-credential -UserName $env:USERNAME -Message "Using Windows Authentication. Please enter your windows credentials."
 17  New-NavContainer -accept_eula:$accept_eula `
 18                   -containername $containername `
 19                   -auth windows `
 20                   -Credential $credential `
 21                   -includeCSide `
 22                   -alwaysPull `
 23                   -doNotExportObjectsToText `
 24                   -usessl:$false `
 25                   -updateHosts `
 26                   -assignPremiumPlan `
 27                   -shortcuts Desktop `
 28                   -imageName $navdockerimage `
 29                   -additionalParameters $additionalParameters
 30
 31  Setup-NavContainerTestUsers -containerName $containername -password $credential.Password
 32
```

Press *F5* to run the script and wait. In the console pane, you can see the installation log, and when the script has finished creating your container, you'll have all the information needed for connecting to your local Dynamics 365 Business Central environment:

```
Starting Internet Information Server
Creating Self Signed Certificate
Self Signed Certificate Thumbprint 976CE96F4F6E3DE8343B725819D453766E77227E
Modifying Service Tier Config File with Instance Specific Settings
Starting NAV Service Tier
Creating DotNetCore Web Server Instance
Enabling Financials User Experience
Creating http download site
Creating Windows user admin
Setting SA Password and enabling SA
Creating admin as SQL User and add to sysadmin
Creating SUPER user
Container IP Address: 172.19.98.95
Container Hostname   : D365BC
Container Dns Name   : D365BC
Web Client           : http://D365BC/NAV/
Dev. Server          : http://D365BC
Dev. ServerInstance  : NAV

Files:
http://D365BC:8080/al-0.15.18771.vsix

Initialization took 41 seconds
Ready for connections!
```

These details are what you have to provide in the `launch.json` file in Visual Studio Code for connecting to your environment for developing extensions (as explained in `Chapter 3`, *Modern Development Environment Overview*). The `.vsix` link file is the AL Extension that you need to install in Visual Studio Code for having the AL language support and downloading symbols from Business Central:

The installation will also place on your desktop the links for connecting to web client, Windows client, C/SIDE, Powershell prompt in the container, and Command Prompt in the container.

# Manually creating a sandbox based on Docker

You can also create a Dynamics 365 Business Central sandbox environment without using the sandbox links to the Business Central production tenant, but instead using custom scripts for creating Docker-based sandboxes hosted locally or on Azure Container Instances.

# Steps for manually creating a locally hosted Dynamics 365 Business Central sandbox

After installing Docker for Windows on your local machine, you can manually create a Docker-based Dynamics 365 Business Central container by running a script that pulls a container image from the Docker hub.

From Command Prompt, you can execute the following command:

```
docker run -m 4G -e ACCEPT_EULA=Y -e UseSSL=N microsoft/bcsandbox:latest
```

This will create a Dynamics 365 Business Central container with the latest image available.

If you want to create a sandbox with a particular localization (for example, IT), you can run the following command:

```
docker run -m 4G -e ACCEPT_EULA=Y -e UseSSL=N microsoft/bcsandbox:it
```

 When executing this command, Docker pulls the container image from Docker hub with all the dependent layers. This will take some time, and it requires at least 15 GB free space available on the disk.

When the container provisioning is finished, you can see your running Docker containers by executing the following command:

```
docker ps
```

And this is the output of this command:

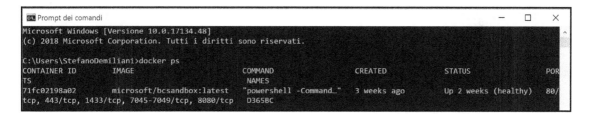

Other useful Docker commands to know are the following ones:

- `docker images`: Returns the container list
- `docker pull`: Docker image download (layers not in use)

- `docker rmi`: Removes a docker image via the ID
- `docker run`: Runs a docker image
- `docker ps`: Shows the running container
- `docker rm`: Removes a container ( `-f`, if it's running)
- `docker inspect`: Shows the content of a container (JSON)
- `docker logs`: Shows the execution log for a container
- `Docker start/stop/restart <containername>`
- Docker commit: Save the current status of a stopped container as a new container image

You can find more details about Docker commands from the following link: `https://docs.docker.com/engine/reference/commandline/docker/`.

In addition to using standard Docker commands, the NAV team provides an interesting PowerShell module called `navcontainerhelper`. This is a module from the PowerShell gallery that contains a number of PowerShell functions, which help running and interacting with NAV containers.

To use this module, start PowerShell ISE as administrator and run the following:

```
install-module navcontainerhelper -force
```

After installation, you can have a list of available commands by executing the following:

```
Get-command -Module navcontainerhelper
```

To create a new Dynamics 365 Business Central container, run the following script:

```
$imageName = "microsoft/bcsandbox:latest"
$navcredential = New-Object System.Management.Automation.PSCredential -
argumentList "admin", (ConvertTo-SecureString -String "P@ssword1" -
AsPlainText -Force)
New-NavContainer -accept_eula `
        -containerName "D365BC" `
        -Auth NavUserPassword `
        -imageName $imageName `
        -Credential $navcredential' '
```

This will create a locally hosted container based on the latest Dynamics 365 Business Central image with a specified name (`D365BC`) and `NavUserPassword` as authentication (with provided credentials):

This Powershell module is also useful for creating a new NAV container with your database backup:

```
$imageName = "microsoft/dynamics-nav:2018"
$navcredential = New-Object System.Management.Automation.PSCredential -
argumentList "admin", (ConvertTo-SecureString -String "P@ssword1" -
AsPlainText -Force)
New-NavContainer -accept_eula `
        -containerName "test" `
        -Auth NavUserPassword `
        -imageName $imageName `
        -Credential $navcredential `
        -licenseFile
"https://www.dropbox.com/stefano/abcdefghijkl/my.flf?dl=1" `
        -additionalParameters @('--env
```

```
bakfile="https://www.dropbox.com/s/abcdefghijkl/Demo%20Database%20NAV%20%28
11-0%29.bak?dl=1"')
```

You can find more information about `navcontainerhelper` from the following links:

- `https://github.com/Microsoft/navcontainerhelper`
- `https://blogs.msdn.microsoft.com/freddyk/tag/navcontainerhelper/`

# Steps for manually creating an Azure Container Instance-based Dynamics 365 Business Central sandbox

A Docker container can also be provisioned in the Azure cloud by using **Azure Container Instances**. **Azure Container Instances** (**ACI**) provide a simple way to provision a container in Azure without installing everything. An Azure Container Instance is a single container that starts in seconds and is billed by the time (number of seconds) you use it.

You can create a new ACI directly from the Azure portal by selecting **New** | **Azure Container Instance** and then providing a resource group and the Docker image to start creating the container:

My recommendation is instead to use the **Azure Command Line Interface** (**CLI**) that you can start directly from the top bar of your Azure portal:

From here, you can create a new ACI (container on Azure) by executing the following steps and commands:

**Step 1**: Create a resource group:

```
az group create --name D365BCRG --location WestEurope
```

**Step 2**: Create the container with the Dynamics 365 Business Central image you want (here I've selected the latest):

```
az container create -g D365BCRG -n d365bc --image
microsoft/bcsandbox:latest --os-type Windows --cpu 2 --memory 4 --ip-
address public -e ACCEPT_EULA=Y USESSL=N ClickOnce=Y
publicDnsName=d365bcpackt.westeurope.azurecontainer.io --dns-name-label
d365bcpackt --ports 80 7046 7047 7049 8080
```

 The DNS name (in this sample is d365bcpackt) must be unique to the region.

**Step 3 (optional)**: To monitor the container setup process, you can execute the following command:

```
az container attach -g D365BCRG -n d365bcpackt
```

The user and the password for connecting to your just-deployed container can be found on the log by using this command:

```
az container logs --resource-group D365BCRG --name d365bc
```

When the ACI provisioning is complete, you can connect to your Dynamics 365 Business Central container running on Azure by using the public DNS name.

More information about Azure container instances can be found here: `https://azure.microsoft.com/en-us/services/container-instances/`.

# Summary

In this chapter, we saw the various options for creating a sandbox environment for working and developing with Dynamics 365 Business Central. This is the starting point for a development environment, where we can connect with Visual Studio Code, publish, deploy, and debug extensions.

In `Chapter 5`, *Developing an Extension with AL and VS CODE*, we'll see how to create a real-world extension for Dynamics 365 Business Central by using the AL language and Visual Studio Code.

# Developing an Extension with AL and VS Code

In Chapter 4, *Creating Your Development Sandbox*, we saw how to create a Microsoft Dynamics 365 Business Central sandbox environment for developing and testing purposes, and we saw all the available sandbox types you can create (online, hosted on Azure, and hosted locally).

In this chapter, we'll develop a complete extension for Microsoft Dynamics 365 Business Central by using the new modern development environment, Visual Studio Code.

Here, you will learn the following:

- How to create new tables and extend existing ones
- How to create new pages and extend existing ones
- How to create custom business logic and how to use events in AL
- How to create a custom report
- Different tips and tricks for developing extensions with AL
- Handling dependencies between extensions
- Handling translations and multi-language capabilities

## The business case

As a business case for our brand new extension for Microsoft Dynamics 365 Business Central, we need to handle the categorization of customers and we need to handle some sales business processes according to the customer's category.

We need to define categories for customers and we need to have a field on the customer card to associate a category with a customer. We need a way to define a default category and assign this default category to a particular customer or to all customers.

Then, for each customer category, we can define whether this category has the possibility to receive gifts when the customer that belongs to that category makes a sales order for an item. For that, we need to have a table set up where for each customer category, we can associate an item with a minimum quantity to order and the associated quantity for a free gift. For example, we need to setup a record such as this:

| Customer category | Item no. | Minimum quantity on order | Gift quantity |
|---|---|---|---|
| GOLD | ITEM001 | 5 | 1 |

Here, if a customer that belongs to the GOLD category makes a sales order with ITEM001 with quantity >= 5, they will receive a gift with ITEM001 with a quantity of 1.

When entering the sales order line in Microsoft Dynamics 365 Business Central, if there's a match between the customer category, the item on the sales line, and the minimum quantity, the system must add a new line with the gift and the 100% discount automatically.

 This is only a sample to demonstrate different features when developing an extension. We could certainly improve the controls and the business logic but that is outside our scope here.

By analyzing the business case, we can see that we need to:

- Add two new tables to Microsoft Dynamics 365 Business Central (Customer Category and Free Gifts)
- Modify existing tables (the Customer table)
- Create new pages (the UI for our custom objects)
- Modify existing pages (such as Customer Card)
- Create new business logic (custom codeunits)

After opening Visual Studio Code (with the AL language module for Microsoft Dynamics 365 Business Central enabled) we can start a new AL project (**AL:Go!** in Command Palette). In launch.json, we can enter the connection details into our sandbox environment (as shown in Chapter 4, *Creating Your Development Sandbox*) and with **AL: Download Symbols** we can download the symbols.

Now, we're ready to develop our extension for Microsoft Dynamics 365 Business Central.

# Developing the extension

We've structured our project folder as follows:

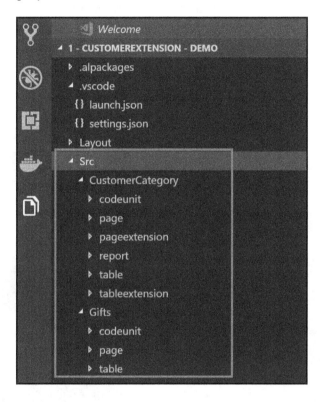

We have an `Src` folder and under that we have a subfolder for every functionality and then for object type.

The name of each AL file is created using Microsoft's naming guidelines:

- Each file name must start with the corresponding type and ID, followed by a dot for full objects or a dash for extensions:
  - **Full objects**: `<Type><Id>.<ObjectName>.al`, such as `Tab.50100.MyTable.al`
  - **Extensions**: `<Type><BaseId>-Ext<ObjectId>.<ObjectName>.al` : `page 50100 MyPage extends Customer Card` such as `Pag21-Ext50100.MyPage.al`

- It is required to use a prefix or suffix for the name property of the fields in your extension. You would then use the `Caption/CaptionML` values for what to display to the user. This avoids the collision of fields between extensions:
  - A tag must be at least three characters
  - The object/field name must start or end with the tag
  - If a conflict arises, the one who registered the tag always wins
  - Example: `SalesPersonCode.SDM`

Our `app.json` file (extension manifest file) is defined as follows:

```
app.json    ✕
 1   {
 2       "id": "3ba9246e-5bb0-4eac-b9ea-5269737fb9cc",
 3       "name": "CustomerExtension",
 4       "publisher": "Stefano Demiliani",
 5       "brief": "My Customer Extension",
 6       "description": "My Customer Extension for D365BC",
 7       "version": "1.0.0.0",
 8       "privacyStatement": "",
 9       "EULA": "",
10       "help": "",
11       "url": "http://www.demiliani.com",
12       "logo": "C:\\Users\\Stefano\\OneDrive\\Immagini\\Avatar.PNG",
13       "capabilities": [],
14       "dependencies": [],
15       "screenshots": [],
16       "platform": "12.0.0.0",
17       "application": "12.0.0.0",
18       "idRange": {
19         "from": 50100,
20         "to": 50149
21       }
22   }
```

# Creating the new tables

As our first step, we need to create the two new tables that we need to add to Dynamics 365 Business Central in order to satisfy our requirements.

To create a new table, we add a file under the `Src\CustomerCategory\table` folder called `Tab50100.CustomerCategory.al`, and in this file we create the definition for the `Customer Category` table by using the `ttable` AL snippet:

```al
0 references
table id MyTable
{
    DataClassification = ToBeClassified;

    fields
    {
        1 reference
        field(1;MyField; Integer)
        {

            DataClassification = ToBeClassified;
        }
    }

    keys
    {
        - reference
        key(PK; MyField)
        {
            Clustered = true;
        }
    }

    var
        0 references
        myInt: Integer;

    trigger OnInsert()
    begin

    end;

    trigger OnModify()
    begin

    end;

    trigger OnDelete()
    begin

    end;
```

The snippet adds a skeleton to create a table. Here, you need to set the object ID, the object name, and define the fields of your tables and keys.

Our Customer Category table will be defined as follows:

```al
Tab50100.CustomerCategory.al  ×

8 references
table 50100 "Customer Category"|
{
    DrillDownPageId = "Customer Category List";
    LookupPageId = "Customer Category List";
    Caption='Customer Category';

    fields
    {
        7 references
        field(1; No; Code[20])
        {
            DataClassification = CustomerContent;
            Caption = 'No.';
            trigger OnValidate();
            begin

            end;
        }
        2 references
        field(2; Description; Text[50])
        {
            DataClassification = CustomerContent;
            CaptionML = ENU = 'Description', ITA = 'Descrizione';
        }
        5 references
        field(3; Default; Boolean)
        {
            DataClassification = CustomerContent;
            Caption = 'Default';
        }
        1 reference
        field(4; TotalCustomersForCategory; Integer)
        {
            FieldClass = FlowField;
            CalcFormula = count (Customer where ("Customer Category" = field (No)));
            CaptionML = ENU = 'Total customers for category', ITA = 'Nr. clienti nella categoria';
        }

        0 references
        field(5; EnableNewsletter; Option)
        {
            OptionMembers = " ","Full","Limited";
```

Here is the complete AL code:

```
table 50100 "Customer Category"
{
    DrillDownPageId = "Customer Category List";
    LookupPageId = "Customer Category List";
    Caption='Customer Category';
    fields
    {
        field(1; No; Code[20])
        {
            DataClassification = CustomerContent;
            Caption = 'No.';
            trigger OnValidate();
            begin
            end;
        }
        field(2; Description; Text[50])
        {
            DataClassification = CustomerContent;
            Caption = 'Description';
        }

        field(3; Default; Boolean)
        {
            DataClassification = CustomerContent;
            Caption = 'Default';
        }

        field(4; TotalCustomersForCategory; Integer)
        {
            FieldClass = FlowField;
            CalcFormula = count (Customer where ("Customer Category" =
             field (No)));
            Caption = 'Total customers for category';
        }

        field(5; EnableNewsletter; Option)
        {
            OptionMembers = " ","Full","Limited";
            OptionCaption = ' ,Full,Limited';
            Caption = 'Enable Newsletter';
            DataClassification = CustomerContent;
        }

        field(6; FreeGiftsAvailable; Boolean)
        {
            DataClassification = CustomerContent;
```

```
                Caption = 'Free Gifts Available';
        }
    }
    keys
    {
        key(PK; No)
        {
            Clustered = true;
        }
    }
}
```

 The `DrillDownPageId` and `LookupPageId` properties must obviously be set after creating the relative pages.

In this table's definition we have:

- `TotalCustomersForCategory` is a `FlowField` that counts the number of customers associated with this category code
- `EnableNewsletter` is an option field (the option values are defined in the `OptionMembers` property)
- The `DataClassification` property is set to `CustomerContent` for all fields (please never leave the default `ToBeClassified` value)

We have to take the same steps to define the `Free Gifts` table (the `Tab50101.FreeGifts.al` file).

Here is the complete AL code for this table definition:

```
table 50101 "FreeGifts"
{
    DataClassification = CustomerContent;
    DrillDownPageId = "Free Gift List";
    LookupPageId = "Free Gift List";
    Caption='Free Gifts';

    fields
    {
        field(1; CustomerCategoryCode; Code[20])
        {
            DataClassification = CustomerContent;
            TableRelation = "Customer Category";
            Caption = 'Customer Category Code';
        }
```

```
        field(2; ItemNo; Code[20])
        {
            DataClassification = CustomerContent;
            TableRelation = Item;
            Caption = 'Item No.';
        }

        field(3; MinimumOrderQuantity; Decimal)
        {
            DataClassification = CustomerContent;
            Caption = 'Minimum Order Quantity';
        }

        field(4; GiftQuantity; Decimal)
        {
            DataClassification = CustomerContent;
            Caption = 'Free Gift Quantity';
        }
    }

    keys
    {
        key(PK; CustomerCategoryCode, ItemNo)
        {
            Clustered = true;
        }
    }
}
```

In this table definition:

- The key for the Free Gifts table is a composite key (the CustomerCategoryCode and ItemNo fields)
- The CustomerCategoryCode field is related to the Customer Category table (previously defined)
- The ItemNo field is related to the Item table

# Creating the pages for the new tables

After the creation of these two new tables, we need to create the pages for the user interface in order to access those tables (and set them as LookupPageID and DrillDownPageId for the tables, as previously described).

To create a new **List** page for the Customer Category table, we select the Src\CustomerCategory\page folder and add a file called Pag50100.CustomerCategoryList.al. In this file, we can use the tpage snippet, and we select the second one proposed (Page of type list):

```
1    tpage
2        ☐ tpage, Page                              Snippet: Page of type list (AL Languag ×
3        ☐ tpage, Page of type list                  e)
4        ☐ tpage (CRS)
5        ☐ tpagecust                                page Id PageName
6        ☐ tpagecust (CRS)                          {
7        ☐ tpageext                                     PageType = List;
8        ☐ tpageext (CRS)                               SourceTable = TableName;
9        ☐ tpagefield
10       ☐ tpagefield (CRS)                             layout
11       ☐ tpagelist (CRS)                              {
12       ☐ tpagesetup (CRS)                                 area(content)
13       ☐ tpagewizard (CRS: 3 steps)                       {
```

We define the Customer Category List page as follows:

```
1
     2 references
2    page 50100 "Customer Category List"
3    {
4        PageType = List;
5        SourceTable = "Customer Category";
6        UsageCategory = Lists; //To be inserted in Search
7        //CaptionML = ENU = 'Customer Category List', ITA = 'Lista Categorie Cliente';
8        Caption = 'Customer Category List';
9
10       layout
11       {
             0 references
12           area(content)
13           {
                 0 references
14               repeater(Group)
15               {
                     0 references
16                   field(No; No)
17                   {
18                       ApplicationArea = All;
19                   }
                     0 references
20                   field(Description; Description)
21                   {
22                       ApplicationArea = All;
23                   }
                     0 references
24                   field(Default; Default)
25                   {
26                       ApplicationArea = All;
27                   }
28
                     0 references
29                   field(TotalCustomersForCategory; TotalCustomersForCategory)
30                   {
31                       ApplicationArea = All;
32                       ToolTip='Total Customers for Category';
33                   }
34
35                   //Campo con SourceExpression una funzione definita in una codeunit
36                   //field(TEST;cu.TEST)
37                   //{
38                   //    Editable = false;
39                   //}
40
41               }
42           }
             0 references
43           area(factboxes)
44           {
45           }
46   }
```

Here:

- `PageType` is set as List.
- `SourceTable` is set to the table bound to the list (the `Customer Category` table).

- The `UsageCategory` property is used in order to have the page listed when searching in Business Central.
- The `ApplicationArea` property sets the application area that applies to the control. If the control applies to all application areas, you can set the property to `All` and this means that the control will always appear in the user interface. For more informations about `ApplicationArea`, check out this link: `https://docs.microsoft.com/en-us/dynamics365/business-central/dev-itpro/developer/properties/devenv-applicationarea-property`.

In this `Customer Category List` page, we want to add a button for creating default `Customer Category Code` (if not yet created). To do so, in the `actions` area, we add a new action called `Create Default Category` with the following lines of code:

```
action("Create Default Category")
{
    Image = CreateForm;
    Promoted = true;
    PromotedCategory = Process;
    PromotedIsBig = true;
    ApplicationArea = All;
    ToolTip = 'Create default category';
    Caption='Create default category';

    trigger OnAction();
    var
        CustManagement: Codeunit "Customer Management";
    begin
        //!Integration event raised
        OnBeforeCreateDefaultCategoryAction(Rec);
        CustManagement.CreateDefaultCategory();
        //!Integration event raised
        OnAfterCreateDefaultCategoryAction(Rec);
    end;
}
}
}

var
    //cu: Codeunit "Customer Management";

[IntegrationEvent(true, true)]
1 reference
local procedure OnBeforeCreateDefaultCategoryAction(var CustomerCategory: Record "Customer Category"
begin
end;

[IntegrationEvent(true, true)]
1 reference
local procedure OnAfterCreateDefaultCategoryAction(var CustomerCategory: Record "Customer Category")
begin
end;
```

At the beginning and the end of category creation (handled in a function in a separate code unit), we trigger *Integration* events that handle the `OnBefore`/`OnAfter` pattern (triggering Integration events could be useful for future extensions that could depend on this one).

An event of type = Integration can be created with the `teventint` AL snippet.

The complete AL definition for this page is as follows:

```
page 50100 "Customer Category List"
{
    PageType = List;
    SourceTable = "Customer Category";
    UsageCategory = Lists; //To be inserted in D365BC Search
    Caption = 'Customer Category List';
    layout
    {
        area(content)
        {
            repeater(Group)
            {
                field(No; No)
                {
                    ApplicationArea = All;
                }
                field(Description; Description)
                {
                    ApplicationArea = All;
                }
                field(Default; Default)
                {
                    ApplicationArea = All;
                }
                field(TotalCustomersForCategory; TotalCustomersForCategory)
                {
                    ApplicationArea = All;
                    ToolTip='Total Customers for Category';
                }
            }
        }

        area(factboxes)
        {
        }
    }

    actions
    {
        area(processing)
```

```
            {
                action("Create Default Category")
                {
                    Image = CreateForm;
                    Promoted = true;
                    PromotedCategory = Process;
                    PromotedIsBig = true;
                    ApplicationArea = All;
                    ToolTip = 'Creates a default Customer Category';
                    Caption='Create default category';

                    trigger OnAction();
                     var
                        CustManagement: Codeunit "Customer Management";
                     begin
                        //!Integration event raised
                        OnBeforeCreateDefaultCategoryAction(Rec);
                        CustManagement.CreatedefaultCategory();
                        //!Integration event raised
                        OnAfterCreateDefaultCategoryAction(Rec);
                     end;
                }
            }
        }
  [IntegrationEvent(true, true)]
  local procedure OnBeforeCreateDefaultCategoryAction(var CustomerCategory:
Record "Customer Category")
  begin
  end;


  [IntegrationEvent(true, true)]
  local procedure OnAfterCreateDefaultCategoryAction(var CustomerCategory:
Record "Customer Category")
  begin
  end;
}
```

We have to do the same to create the `Free Gift List` page (used to insert data when setting up the free gifts for a customer category). This page will be defined as follows:

```
2 references
page 50103 "Free Gift List"
{
    PageType = List;
    SourceTable = FreeGifts;
    UsageCategory = Lists; //Per poterla inserire nel Search
    CaptionML=ENU='Free Gift Setup',ITA='Free Gift Setup';

    layout
    {
        0 references
        area(content)
        {
            0 references
            repeater(Group)
            {
                0 references
                field(CustomerCategoryCode; CustomerCategoryCode)
                {
                    ApplicationArea = All;
                }
                0 references
                field(ItemNo; ItemNo)
                {
                    ApplicationArea = All;
                }
                0 references
                field(MinimumOrderQuantity; MinimumOrderQuantity)
                {
                    ApplicationArea = All;
                    Style = Strong;
                }
                0 references
                field(GiftQuantity;GiftQuantity)
                {
                    ApplicationArea = All;
                    Style = Strong;
                }
            }
        }
        0 references
        area(factboxes)
        {
```

And here is the complete AL code:

```
page 50103 "Free Gift List"
{
    PageType = List;
    SourceTable = FreeGifts;
    UsageCategory = Lists;
    Caption='Free Gift Setup';
    layout
    {
        area(content)
        {
            repeater(Group)
            {
                field(CustomerCategoryCode; CustomerCategoryCode)
                {
                    ApplicationArea = All;
                }
                field(ItemNo; ItemNo)
                {
                    ApplicationArea = All;
                }
                field(MinimumOrderQuantity; MinimumOrderQuantity)
                {
                    ApplicationArea = All;
                    Style = Strong;
                }
                field(GiftQuantity;GiftQuantity)
                {
                    ApplicationArea = All;
                    Style = Strong;
                }
            }
        }
    }
}
```

# Extending standard Dynamics 365 Business Central objects (tables and pages)

After defining (and creating) the new objects that we need to add to Dynamics 365 Business Central with our extension, we now need to modify the existing ones (standard objects from Microsoft). We previously defined the `Customer Category` table and we now need to do the following:

- Add a field to the standard `Customer` table (called `Customer Category Code`) in order to associate a `Customer` with a `Customer Category`
- Show this newly added field on the standard `Customer Card object`
- Add a `Customer Category` field to the Item Ledger Entry table for statistical purposes (it will be filled when posting a sales order)

With Dynamics 365 Business Central and the new extension model, it's not possible to directly modify a standard object, so instead you need to extend it.

To add a custom field to the standard Dynamics 365 Business Central (or change some properties in a standard table), you need to create a `tableextension` object. To add a custom field to a standard page (or change some properties of a standard page), you need to create a `pageextension` object.

The standard AL snipping tool to create a `tableextension` object is `ttableext`:

It has the following schema:

```
tableextension Id MyExtension extends MyTargetTable
{
    fields
    {
        // Add changes to table fields here
    }
    var
        myInt: Integer;
}
```

In our `tableextension`, we extend the `Customer` table by adding a new custom field, so we go to the `Src\CustomerCategory\tableextension` folder and create a new AL file called `Tab18-Ext50100.CustomerTableExtensions.al`.

Here:

- We add a new field called `Customer Category SDM` (we add our suffix in order to be unique) with `ID = 50100` to the `Customer` table
- We set the table relation of this field to the `Customer Category` table

The AL code of this `tableextension` object is as follows:

```
tableextension 50100 "CustomerTableExtensions" extends Customer
{
    fields
    {
        field(50100; "Customer Category SDM"; Code[20])
        {
            TableRelation = "Customer Category".No;
            Caption='Customer Category Code';
            DataClassification = CustomerContent;
        }
    }
}
```

The `tableextension` for the `Item Ledger Entry` table is defined as follows (in the `Tab32-Ext50101.ItemLedgerEntryExtension.al` file):

```
tableextension 50101 ItemLedgerEntryExtension extends "Item Ledger Entry"
{
        fields
    {
        field(50100;"Customer Category SDM";Code[20])
        {
            TableRelation = "Customer Category".No;
```

```
        Caption = 'Customer Category';
    }
  }
}
```

Remember that in `tableextension` objects, you can create new keys (with fields added from your extension) but you cannot modify the existing keys in the standard table. You can also modify some properties of standard fields (very limited!) with the following syntax:

```
tableextension 50101 ItemLedgerEntryExtension extends "Item Ledger Entry"
{
    fields
    {

        1 reference
        field(50100;"Customer Category";Code[20])
        {
            TableRelation = "Customer Category".No;
            Description = 'Customer Category';
            Caption = 'Customer Category';

        }


        modify("Document No.")
        {
            Caption = 'Document No.';

        }
    }
}
```

AccessByPermission
AutoFormatExpression
AutoFormatType
AutoIncrement
BlankNumbers
BlankZero
CalcFormula
Caption
CaptionClass
CaptionML
CharAllowed
ClosingDates

AccessByPermission property                          ×

Sets a value for a table field or UI element that
determines the permission mask for an object that
a user must have to see and access the related
page fields or UI element in the client. The UI
element will be removed at runtime if the user
does not have permissions to a certain object as
specified in the Access By Permission window..

All types of UI elements will be removed if they
relate to an object to which the user does not have
the required permissions:

Now, we need to modify the standard Customer Card page. The standard AL snippet to create a pageextension object is tpageext:

It has this syntax:

```
pageextension Id MyExtension extends MyTargetPage
{
    layout
    {
        // Add changes to page layout here
    }
    actions
    {
        // Add changes to page actions here
    }
    var
        myInt: Integer;
}
```

We go to the Src\CustomerCategory\pageextension folder, we create a new AL file called Pag21-Ext50102.CustomerCardExtension.al, and with the tpageext snippet we create the following page extension.

Here:

- We extend the Customer Card standard page.
- We add the Customer Category field as the last field of the **General** tab.

- In the **Action** section, we had a custom action button called **Assign Default Category** that will assign the default `Customer Category` to this `Customer` (the code will be placed in the `OnAction` trigger). To handle the business logic (code) inside this `OnAction` trigger, we'll create a `Codeunit` that contains the business logic for our extension (defined in the *Writing the custom business logic (Codeunit)* section) and here we do the following:
  - Create a reference for this `Codeunit` (called `Customer Management`)
  - Call a function defined in this `Codeunit` (called `AssignDefaultCategory`) that performs the action we want

The complete `pageextension` code is as follows:

```
pageextension 50102 "CustomerCardExtension" extends "Customer Card"
{
    layout
    {
        addlast(General)
        {
            field("Customer Category SDM"; "Customer Category SDM")
            {
                ToolTip = 'Customer Category';
                ApplicationArea = All; //Always add this!
            }
        }
    }
    actions
    {
        addlast("Functions")
        {
            action("Assign default category")
            {
                Image = ChangeCustomer;
                Promoted = true;
                PromotedCategory = Process;
                PromotedIsBig = true;
                ApplicationArea = All;
                Caption = 'Assign Default Category';
                ToolTip = 'Assigns the default category for the
                selected customer';

                trigger OnAction();
                var
                    CustManagement: Codeunit "Customer Management";
                begin
                    CustManagement.AssignDefaultCategory(Rec."No.");
```

```
                                    end;
                     }
              }
         }
    }
```

The action we've added has an associated *Image* (you can choose the images by name) and it's a *promoted* action (you can see it in the **Home ribbon** section in the Customer Card). Here, we should also handle the OnBefore/OnAfter integration event if we want to permit integration with other extensions.

We also create a pageextension for the Customer List in order to add a new action to perform a massive update of the Customer Category field for all Customers (default category for all):

```al
0 references
pageextension 50103 CustomerListExtension extends "Customer List"
{

    actions
    {
        addlast(Processing)
        {
            0 references
            action("Assign Default Category")
            {
                Image = ChangeCustomer;
                Promoted = true;
                PromotedCategory = Process;
                PromotedIsBig = true;
                ApplicationArea = All;
                Caption = 'Assign Default Category to all Customers';
                ToolTip = 'Assigns the Default Category to all Customers';

                trigger OnAction();
                var
                    CustManagement: Codeunit "Customer Management";
                begin
                    CustManagement.AssignDefaultCategory();
                end;
            }
        }
    }
}
```

# Writing the custom business logic (Codeunit)

Now, it's time to write the business logic code.

As a best practice (`https://community.dynamics.com/nav/w/designpatterns`), we don't want to have code inside tables or pages so here we create two Codeunit objects:

- **Customer Management Codeunit**: Contains all the business logic related to managing the Customer and Customer Category
- **Free Gift Management Codeunit**: Contains all the business logic related to managing the Free Gift process

To create these Codeunits, we create two new AL files in the `Src\CustomerCategory\codeunit` and `Src\Gifts\codeunit` folders with the names of `Cod50100.CustomerManagement.al` and `Cod50101.FreeGiftManagement.al`, respectively.

We use the `tcodeunit` snipper to create a new empty `Codeunit`:

The snippet has the following structure:

```
codeunit Id MyCodeunit
{
    trigger OnRun()
    begin
    end;
    var
        myInt: Integer;
}
```

Inside a codeunit, we can have the standard OnRun() trigger and we can define *procedures* (global or local) or *events*. A procedure with the *local* prefix is local to the objects where it is defined (no visible to external objects).

Our Customer Management Codeunit will be defined as follows:

```al
Cod50100.CustomerManagement.al  ●

    1 reference
1   codeunit 50100 "Customer Management"
2   {
3
4
5       trigger OnRun();
6       begin
7       end;
8
9
        1 reference
10      procedure AssignDefaultCategory(CustomerCode: Code[20])
11
12      var
13          Customer : Record Customer;
14          CustomerCategory : Record "Customer Category";
15      begin
16          //Set default category for a Customer
17          Customer.Get(CustomerCode);
18          CustomerCategory.SetRange(Default,true);
19          if CustomerCategory.FindFirst() then
20          begin
21              Customer."Customer Category" := CustomerCategory.No;
22              Customer.Modify();
23          end;
24      end;
25
        0 references
26      procedure AssignDefaultCategory()
27      var
28          Customer : Record Customer;
29          CustomerCategory : Record "Customer Category";
30      begin
31          //Set default category for ALL Customer
32          CustomerCategory.SetRange(Default,true);
33          if CustomerCategory.FindFirst() then
34          begin
35              if Customer.FindSet() then
36              repeat
37                  Customer."Customer Category" := CustomerCategory.No;
38                  Customer.Modify();
39              until Customer.Next()=0;
40          end;
41      end;
```

Here is the complete AL code:

```
codeunit 50100 "Customer Management"
{
    trigger OnRun();
    begin
    end;
    procedure AssignDefaultCategory(CustomerCode: Code[20])
    var
        Customer : Record Customer;
        CustomerCategory : Record "Customer Category";
    begin
        //Set default category for a Customer
        Customer.Get(CustomerCode);
        CustomerCategory.SetRange(Default,true);
        if CustomerCategory.FindFirst() then
        begin
            Customer."Customer Category" := CustomerCategory.No;
            Customer.Modify();
        end;
    end;

    procedure AssignDefaultCategory()
    var
        Customer : Record Customer;
        CustomerCategory : Record "Customer Category";
    begin
        //Set default category for ALL Customer
        CustomerCategory.SetRange(Default,true);
        if CustomerCategory.FindFirst() then
        begin
            if Customer.FindSet() then
            repeat
                Customer."Customer Category" := CustomerCategory.No;
                Customer.Modify();
            until Customer.Next()=0;
        end;
    end;

    procedure CreateDefaultCategory()
    var
        CustomerCategory: Record "Customer Category";
    begin
        CustomerCategory.No := 'DEFAULT';
        CustomerCategory.Description := 'Default Customer Category';
        CustomerCategory.Default := true;
        if CustomerCategory.Insert then;
    end;
```

```
//Returns the number of Customers without an assigned Customer Category
procedure GetTotalCustomersWithoutCategory(): Integer
var
    Customer: record Customer;
begin
    Customer.SetRange("Customer Category",'');
    exit(customer.Count());
end;


}
```

Here:

- We have a function called `AssignDefaultCategory` that has two definitions (overloading):
  - If no parameters are passed, the function assigns the `Customer Category` set as the default one to `ALL Customers` in the database
  - If `Customer Code` is passed, the function assigns the `Customer Category` set as the default one to this `Customer`
- We have a function called `CreateDefaultCategory` that creates a default `Customer Category` record
- We have a function called `GetTotalCustomersWithoutCategory` that returns the number of customers where the category is not assigned

The second `Codeunit` that we need to create is for handling the gift process when a user enters a sales order for a customer. We mainly need to create a function that, when a user enters a sales line for a customer, checks for the category assigned to this customer and whether there's an associated free gift for the item they're buying. If so, the system must insert a new line in the sales line table for this order with the item and with the line discount is equal to 100%. We can do that by using events and subscribing to standard events triggered by Dynamics 365 Business Central.

The `Free Gift Management Codeunit` is defined as follows:

```
Cod50101.FreeGiftManagement.al ●
      0 references
   1  codeunit 50101 "FreeGiftManagement"
   2  {
   3      [EventSubscriber(ObjectType::Table, 37, 'OnAfterValidateEvent', 'Quantity', false, false)]
      0 references
   4      local procedure AddFreeGift(var Rec: Record "Sales Line")
   5      var
   6          FreeGift: Record FreeGifts;
   7          SalesLine: Record "Sales Line";
   8          Customer: Record Customer;
   9      begin
  10          //if (Rec.Type = Rec.Type::Item) and (IsCustomerGOLD(Rec."Sell-to Customer No.")) then begin
  11          if (Rec.Type = Rec.Type::Item) and (Customer.Get(Rec."Sell-to Customer No.")) then begin
  12          if FreeGift.Get(Customer."Customer Category", Rec."No.") and (rec.Quantity > FreeGift.MinimumOrderQuantity) then begin
  13              //Integration event raised
  14              OnBeforeFreeGiftSalesLineAdded(Rec);
  15              //Creates a new Sales Line with the gift
  16              SalesLine.init;
  17              SalesLine.TransferFields(Rec);
  18              SalesLine."Line No." := Rec."Line No." + 10000;
  19              SalesLine.Validate(Quantity, FreeGift.GiftQuantity);
  20              SalesLine.Validate("Line Discount %", 100);
  21              if SalesLine.Insert() then;
  22              //Integration Eent raised
  23              OnAfterFreeGiftSalesLineAdded(Rec, SalesLine);
  24          end;
  25
  26          end;
  27      end;
  28
  29
  30      [IntegrationEvent(true, true)]
      1 reference
  31      local procedure OnBeforeFreeGiftSalesLineAdded(var Rec: Record "Sales Line")
  32      begin
  33      end;
  34
  35      [IntegrationEvent(true, true)]
      1 reference
  36      local procedure OnAfterFreeGiftSalesLineAdded(var Rec: Record "Sales Line"; var SalesLineGift: Record "Sales Line")
  37      begin
  38      end;
  39
  40      [EventSubscriber(ObjectType::Table, 32, 'OnAfterInsertEvent', '', false, false)]
```

And here is the complete AL code:

```
codeunit 50101 "FreeGiftManagement"
{
    [EventSubscriber(ObjectType::Table, 37, 'OnAfterValidateEvent',
'Quantity', false, false)]
    local procedure AddFreeGift(var Rec: Record "Sales Line")
    var
        FreeGift: Record FreeGifts;
        SalesLine: Record "Sales Line";
        Customer: Record Customer;
    begin
            if (Rec.Type = Rec.Type::Item) and (Customer.Get(Rec."Sell-to
Customer No.")) then begin
            if FreeGift.Get(Customer."Customer Category", Rec."No.") and
(rec.Quantity > FreeGift.MinimumOrderQuantity) then
            begin
                OnBeforeFreeGiftSalesLineAdded(Rec);
                //Creates a new Sales Line with the free gift
```

```
                        SalesLine.init;
                        SalesLine.TransferFields(Rec);
                        SalesLine."Line No." := Rec."Line No." + 10000;
                        SalesLine.Validate(Quantity, FreeGift.GiftQuantity);
                        SalesLine.Validate("Line Discount %", 100);
                        if SalesLine.Insert() then;
                        OnAfterFreeGiftSalesLineAdded(Rec, SalesLine);
                    end;
                end;
            end;

    [IntegrationEvent(true, true)]
    local procedure OnBeforeFreeGiftSalesLineAdded(var Rec: Record "Sales
Line")
        begin
        end;

    [IntegrationEvent(true, true)]
    local procedure OnAfterFreeGiftSalesLineAdded(var Rec: Record "Sales
Line"; var SalesLineGift: Record "Sales Line")
        begin
        end;

    [EventSubscriber(ObjectType::Table, 32, 'OnAfterInsertEvent', '',
false, false)]
    local procedure OnAfterItemLedgerEntryInsert(var Rec: Record "Item
Ledger Entry")
        var
            Customer: Record Customer;
        begin
            if rec."Entry Type" = rec."Entry Type"::Sale then begin
                if Customer.Get(Rec."Source No.") then begin
                    rec."Customer Category" := Customer."Customer Category";
                    rec.Modify();
                end;
            end;
        end;
}
```

Here:

- With the `teventsub` snippet, we create an event subscriber to the `OnAfterValidate` event of the `Quantity` field for Table 37 (`Sales Line`). This event subscriber is called `AddFreeGift` and here:
    - If the `Sales Line` is of `Type = Item`, we retrieve the customer and its `Customer Category`.

- We check the `Free Gift` table for the `Customer Category` and the `Item No.` in the `Sales Line`.
- If an entry is found (free gift available), we create a new `Sales Line` with the `Item`, the `gift quantity`, and the `Line Discount = 100%`. This code could be placed in a separate Codeunit.
- We trigger Integration events (`OnBeforeFreeGiftSalesLineAdded` and `OnAfterFreeGiftSalesLineAdded`) before and after the new gift line creation (so integration with other extensions are possible).

- We create an `EventSubscriber` function for the `OnAfterInsert` event of Table 32 (`Item Ledger Entry`) in order to copy the `Customer Category Code` to the `Item Ledger Entry` when a sales order is posted. This function is called `OnAfterItemLedgerEntryInsert`.

The main part of our extension is now done.

To be complete, we must provide a translation (see the next section) and a `Permission.xml` file for the specific permission set that our extension must have. The `PermissionSet` definition is as follows:

We now press *Ctrl + Shift + B* (or **AL:Package** in Visual Studio Code Command Palette) to compile our solution:

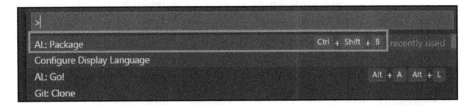

If there are no errors in our Solution, the Extension is compiled and the .app file is created in our project folder:

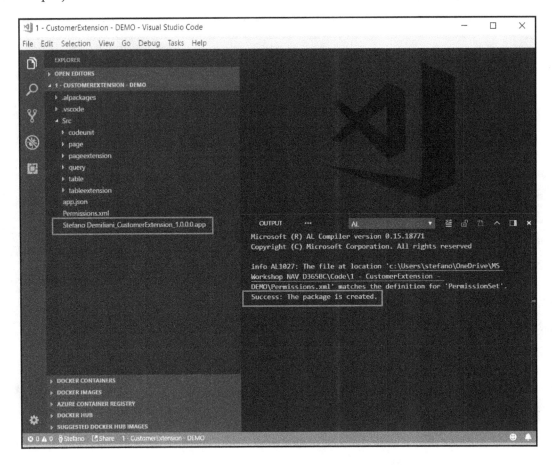

This is the .app extension file that we can deploy on Dynamics 365 Business Central.

We've developed our extension and we're ready to test it. To directly deploy the extension to the Dynamics 365 Business Central sandbox environment from Visual Studio Code, just press *F5* (or **AL:Publish** from the Command Palette):

The extension will be directly published and you can find it on the Extension Management page (with your wonderful logo as defined in the logo property in app.json):

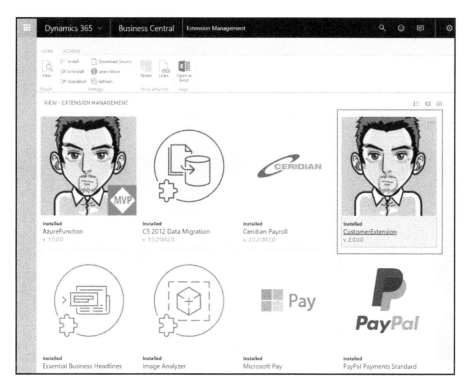

# Handling translations with XLIFF files

Dynamics 365 Business Central is multi-language enabled, which means that you can display the user interface in different languages and you need to support that feature when developing extensions.

With classic NAV development in C/SIDE, you manage the multi-language captions by using the `CaptionML` property: https://docs.microsoft.com/en-us/dynamics-nav/captionml-property.

As you've probably seen, in our previous extension, we haven't managed the translation of the captions that we have in our code. You can't find lines with the `CaptionML` set, for example the following:

```
field(2; Description; Text[50])
    {
        DataClassification = CustomerContent;
        CaptionML = ENU = 'Description', ITA = 'Descrizione';
    }
```

But instead, you'll find the following:

```
field(2; Description; Text[50])
    {
        DataClassification = CustomerContent;
        Caption = 'Description';
    }
```

So, how we do handle multi-language support for our extension?

With Dynamics 365 Business Central, using CaptionML to handle the extension's localization is deprecated. The new way is to use the XLIFF format.

To add a new language to the extension you have built, you must first enable the generation of XLIFF files. The XLIFF file extension is `.xlf` and the generated XLIFF file contains the strings that are specified in properties such as `Caption` and `Tooltip`.

To enable XLIFF file generation (translation file), you need to add the following lines to your `app.json` file:

```
app.json          ●
 1    {
 2      "id": "3ba9246e-5bb0-4eac-b9ea-5269737fb9cc",
 3      "name": "CustomerExtension",
 4      "publisher": "Stefano Demiliani",
 5      "brief": "My Customer Extension",
 6      "description": "My Customer Extension for D365BC",
 7      "version": "1.0.0.0",
 8      "privacyStatement": "",
 9      "EULA": "",
10      "help": "",
11      "url": "http://www.demiliani.com",
12      "logo": "C:\\Users\\Stefano\\OneDrive\\Immagini\\Avatar.PNG",
13      "capabilities": [],
14      "dependencies": [],
15      "screenshots": [],
16      "platform": "12.0.0.0",
17      "application": "12.0.0.0",
18      "features": [
19        "TranslationFile"
20      ],
21      "idRange": {
22        "from": 50100,
23        "to": 50149
24      }
25    }
```

After enabling the generation of the `TranslationFile`, if you compile your extension now, you will find a new folder under your project `tree: Translations`. In this folder, you will find a new file called `<YourExtensionName>.g.xlf`:

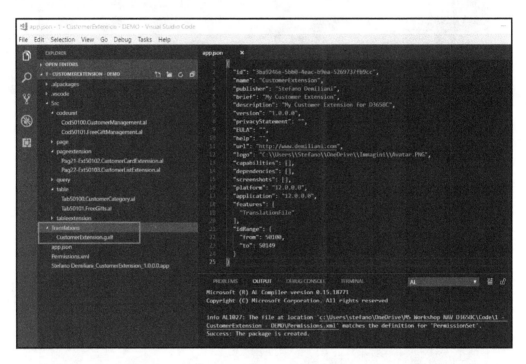

If you open this file (here, it's `CustomerExtension.g.xlf`), you can see an XML file where the source nodes are all the captions that we have in our extension:

This file can be translated in an automatic way using external tools (there are many translation services available on the web for XLIFF files, such as **dynamics translation service** (**DTS**) in LCS Portal), but you can also manually create a translation file in your desired language. If, for example, you want to support Italian localization, just create a new `.xlf` file called `<YourExtensionName>.it-IT.xlf` (by copying the previous `.xlf` file), set the `target-language` to your desired language (for example `it-IT`), and for every source node, add a corresponding target node with the translations:

```xml
CustomerExtension.it-IT.xlf
1  <?xml version="1.0" encoding="utf-8"?>
2  <xliff version="1.2" xmlns="urn:oasis:names:tc:xliff:document:1.2" xmlns:xsi="http://www.w3.org/2001/XMLSchema-instance" xsi:schema
3    <file datatype="xml" source-language="en-US" target-language="it-IT" original="CustomerExtension">
4      <body>
5        <group id="body">
6          <trans-unit id="Table 1530605032 - Property 2879900210" size-unit="char" translate="yes" xml:space="preserve">
7            <source>Customer Category</source>
8            <target>Categoria Cliente</target>
9            <note from="Developer" annotates="general" priority="2" />
10           <note from="Xliff Generator" annotates="general" priority="3">Table:Customer Category - Table:Customer Category</note>
11         </trans-unit>
12         <trans-unit id="Table 1530605032 - Field 949215307 - Property 2879900210" size-unit="char" translate="yes" xml:space="prese
13           <source>No.</source>
14           <target>Codice</target>
15           <note from="Developer" annotates="general" priority="2" />
16           <note from="Xliff Generator" annotates="general" priority="3">Table:Customer Category - Field:No</note>
17         </trans-unit>
18         <trans-unit id="Table 1530605032 - Field 3461834954 - Property 2879900210" size-unit="char" translate="yes" xml:space="pres
19           <source>Description</source>
20           <target>Descrizione</target>
21           <note from="Developer" annotates="general" priority="2" />
22           <note from="Xliff Generator" annotates="general" priority="3">Table:Customer Category - Field:Description</note>
23         </trans-unit>
24         <trans-unit id="Table 1530605032 - Field 1383905037 - Property 2879900210" size-unit="char" translate="yes" xml:space="pres
25           <source>Default</source>
26           <target>Default</target>
27           <note from="Developer" annotates="general" priority="2" />
28           <note from="Xliff Generator" annotates="general" priority="3">Table:Customer Category - Field:Default</note>
29         </trans-unit>
30         <trans-unit id="Table 1530605032 - Field 3907209010 - Property 2879900210" size-unit="char" translate="yes" xml:space="pres
31           <source>Total customers for category</source>
32           <note from="Developer" annotates="general" priority="2" />
33           <note from="Xliff Generator" annotates="general" priority="3">Table:Customer Category - Field:TotalCustomersForCategory</
34         </trans-unit>
```

The **note** tag is useful to place notes about the translation (developer and translator notes).

You have to create an XLIFF file for every language you need to support. For more information about the XLIFF format, you can check out this link: `https://docs.microsoft.com/en-us/dynamics365/business-central/dev-itpro/developer/devenv-work-with-translation-files`.

You can find more informations about the *Microsoft Dynamics 365 Translation Service* at `https://docs.microsoft.com/en-us/dynamics365/unified-operations/dev-itpro/lifecycle-services/translation-service-overview`.

Another useful tool for handling XLIFF files is the *Multilingual App Toolkit Editor*: `https://developer.microsoft.com/en-us/windows/develop/multilingual-app-toolkit`

# Customizing the Headline

The Headline is an interesting new object available in Dynamics 365 Business Central that can be used to immediately show up-to-date information on a Role Center page. A Headline is essentially a page that contains one or more text fields that can be formatted in a particular way. There are nine standard Headlines in Dynamics 365 Business Central:

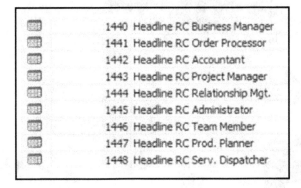

Nine standard Headlines in Dynamics 365 Business Central

A Headline is a page with a new `PageType` called `HeadlinePart`:

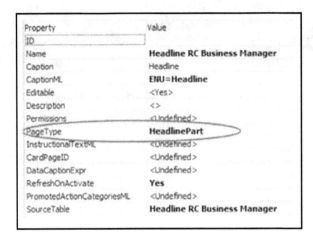

The HeadlinePart Page

For our extension, we also want to customize the Dynamics 365 Business Central Headline (the `Headline RC Business Manager` object) in order to show some statistical information's to users.

> Headlines will only appear in the web client; they will not be shown in other client types.

To create this customization, we need to add a `pageextension` object to our project in order to extend the `Headline RC Business Manager` **page**.

This is the complete code of our `pageextension` for customizing the Headline:

```
pageextension 50104 MyNewBCHeadline extends "Headline RC Business Manager"
{
    layout
    {
        addafter(Control4)
        {
            field(newHeadlineText;newHeadlineText)
            {
                ApplicationArea = all;
                trigger OnDrillDown()
                var
                    Customer: Record Customer;
                    CustomerList: Page "Customer List";
```

```
                begin
                    //Show the customers without category assigned
                    Customer.SetRange("Customer Category",'');
                    CustomerList.SetTableView(Customer);
                    CustomerList.Run();
                end;
            }
        }
    }
    var
        newHeadlineText: Text;
    trigger OnOpenPage()
    var
        HeadlineMgt : Codeunit "Headline Management";
        CustomerManagement: Codeunit "Customer Management";
    begin
        //Set Headline text
        newHeadlineText := 'Number of Customers without assigned Category:
' +
HeadlineMgt.Emphasize(Format(CustomerManagement.GetTotalCustomersWithoutCat
egory()));
    end;
}
```

Here, we add a new headline text (as the last of the actual texts available). In this text, we call the GetTotalCustomersWithoutCategory function (defined in the Customer Management Codeunit in our extension) for retrieving the number of customers without a category assigned. Then we print this text as emphasized by calling the standard Headline Management codeunit in Dynamics 365 Business Central.

We also handle the OnDrillDown event of the headline text field in order to display the record details for the headline message (the details of the customers without an assigned category).

# Developing a custom report for our extension

Now, we want to create a report for our extension that prints the list of Customer Categories, and for every category, the number of associated customers.

To create a report in AL, we need to go to the `Src\CustomerCategory\report` folder and create a new `.al` file called `Rpt50100-CustomerCategoryList.al`. In this file, we use the `treport` snippet to create the report structure:

```
Rpt50100-CustomerCategoryList.al  ●

 1    treport|
 2         □ treport                         Snippet: Report (AL Language)      ×
 3
 4                                           report Id MyReport
 5                                           {
 6                                               dataset
 7                                               {
 8                                                   dataitem(DataItemName;
 9                                           SourceTableName)
10                                                   {
11                                                       column(ColumnName;
12                                           SourceFieldName)
13                                                       {
14
15
16
17
18
19
```

We need to define the report dataset by defining the data item and the associated fields.

In the report definition, we set two properties (`RDLCLayout` and `WordLayout`) that define the folders where the RDLC and word layout for this report are defined (here we have created a `Layout` folder under our project):

In the `OnAfterGetRecord` trigger of the report's data item, we calculate the `FlowField` returning the number of customers associated with the current category. Our report definition is as follows:

```
report 50100 CustomerCategoryList
{
    //DefaultLayout = Word;
    RDLCLayout = 'Layout\CustomerCategoryListRDLC.rdl';
    WordLayout = 'Layout\CustomerCategoryListWord.docx';
    UsageCategory = ReportsAndAnalysis;
    ApplicationArea = All;
    Caption='Customer Category List';
    dataset
    {
        dataitem(CustomerCategory; "Customer Category")
        {
            column(No;No) {}
            column(Description;Description) {}
            column(TotalCustomersForCategory;TotalCustomersForCategory) {}
            column(FreeGiftsAvailable;FreeGiftsAvailable) {}

            trigger OnAfterGetRecord()
            var
            begin
                CalcFields(TotalCustomersForCategory);
            end;
        }
    }
}
```

Now, if we build the report (*Ctrl* + *Shift* + *B*), we can see that in the *Layout* folder we now have two files added (`.rdl` and `.docx`) that are the report layouts:

We can now customize the layout by using standard tools such as Microsoft Word (for Word layout reports) or Report Builder (for RDLC reports).

We can open, for example, the `.rdl` file with SQL Server Report Builder, and from this tool we can see the dataset and its fields and we can customize the layout how we want. From this point, this is exactly the same work as designing a report for Microsoft Dynamics NAV or any other RDLC report in SQL Server:

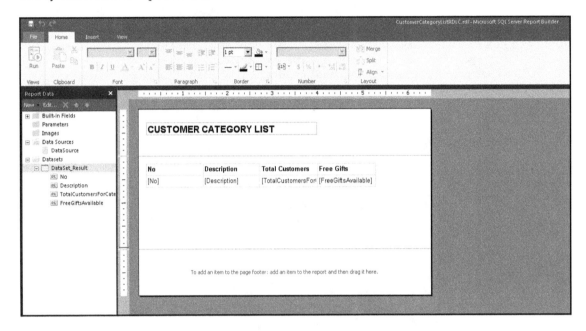

When you publish the extension (by pressing *F5*) to your Sandbox environment, the report and its layout are embedded into the app file and loaded into Dynamics 365 Business Central (`NAV App Object Metadata` table).

# Extension dependency

When developing extensions for Dynamics 365 Business Central, an important architectural aspect when planning for a solution is the extension's *dependency*.

Imagine you have developed and published extension A into your Dynamics 365 Business Central. Extension A adds new tables and pages and extends standard tables and pages. Now you need to create extension B (to handle another set of isolated functionalities), and extension B must interact with tables and fields added from extension A.

If you start developing extension B and try to reference a table defined in extension A, you will receive an error (table is missing because you don't have the symbols from extension A).

Extension B can see entities defined in extension A only if it declares that it depends on extension A.

To see this concept in action, let's create a very simple extension (new project with Visual Studio Code and `AL:Go!`) for adding a new action button to the `Customer Category List` page.

The core part here is in the `app.json` file (manifest). Here, we add a `dependencies` array, and inside this array we need to place the details of the dependent extension (`appId`, `name`, `publisher`, `version`):

```json
app.json    ×
1  {
2      "id": "fd85a2c4-36ac-454b-a5b0-b0a3c3fe8647",
3      "name": "Dependency",
4      "publisher": "Stefano Demiliani",
5      "brief": "",
6      "description": "",
7      "version": "1.0.0.0",
8      "privacyStatement": "",
9      "EULA": "",
10     "help": "",
11     "url": "",
12     "logo": "C:\\Users\\StefanoDemiliani\\OneDrive\\Immagini\\Avatar.PNG",
13     "capabilities": [],
14     "dependencies": [
15         {
16             "appId": "3ba9246e-5bb0-4eac-b9ea-5269737fb9cc",
17             "name": "CustomerExtension",
18             "publisher": "Stefano Demiliani",
19             "version": "1.0.0.0"
20         }
21     ],
22     "screenshots": [],
23     "platform": "12.0.0.0",
24     "application": "12.0.0.0",
25     "features": [
26         "TranslationFile"
27     ],
28     "idRange": {
29         "from": 50100,
30         "to": 50149
31     }
32  }
```

Here:

- appId is the ID of the Customer Management extension previously developed (you can retrieve it from the app.json file)
- name is the name of the Customer Management extension
- publisher is the publisher of the dependent extension
- version is the version number of the dependent extension

After adding the dependencies, if you click *Ctrl + Shift + B* (or **AL:Package**), the symbols of the dependent extension are downloaded (you can see that inside the .alpackages folder) and now you're able to reference all the objects defined in the dependent extension. Obviously, extension A should reside in the database you are programming against.

In our example, we create a pageextension object for extending the Customer Category List page and adding a button for deleting the Customer Category set as default:

The AL code is as follows:

```
pageextension 50108 MyDependentExtension extends "Customer Category List"
{
    actions
```

```
{
    addlast(processing)
    {
        action("Delete Default Category")
        {
            Image = Delete;
            Promoted = true;
            PromotedCategory = Process;
            PromotedIsBig = true;
            ApplicationArea = All;
            Caption = 'Delete Default Category';
            ToolTip = 'Delete the Default Customer Category';

            trigger OnAction();
            var
                CustomerCategory : Record "Customer Category";
                cuCustomer : Codeunit "Customer Management";
            begin
                CustomerCategory.SetRange(Default,true);
                CustomerCategory.Delete();
            end;
        }
    }
}
```

When using extension's dependency, remember these rules:

- When you publish your extensions, you must first publish the extension that are depending on (parent). If you try to publish the extension with the dependency first (child), it will throw an error stating that references do not exist in the database.
- When you remove extensions, you must remove the extensions that have the dependencies first (child).

# Installing and upgrading codeunits

When you develop an extension, there's also an important aspect to take care of: installation and upgrading operations. When an extension is installed or upgraded, you often need to perform certain operations on data, such as populating new data and restoring existing ones. These tasks can be achieved by writing extension-install-and-upgrade code.

In this type of code, you can access the extension properties (such as version, name, publisher, and dependencies) by using the NAVApp.GetCurrentModuleInfo() and NAVAPP.GetModuleInfo() methods.

The install logic can be written by creating an install codeunit, that is, a codeunit with
`SubType = Install`.

An install codeunit has two main system triggers:

- `OnInstallAppPerCompany()`: Includes code for company-related operations.
  Runs once for each company in the database.
- `OnInstallAppPerDatabase()`: Includes code for database-related operations.
  Runs once in the entire install process.

This is an example of an Install `Codeunit` for our previously-developed extension:

```
codeunit 50105 CustomerCategoryInstall
{
    // Subtype = install codeunit.
    Subtype = Install;

    // This trigger includes code for company-related operations.
    trigger OnInstallAppPerCompany();
    var
        archivedVersion : Text;
        CustomerCategory : Record "Customer Category";
    begin
        archivedVersion := NavApp.GetArchiveVersion;
        if archivedVersion = '1.0.0.0' then begin
            NavApp.RestoreArchiveData(Database::"Customer Category");
            NavApp.RestoreArchiveData(Database::Customer);

            NavApp.DeleteArchiveData(Database::"Customer Category");
            NavApp.DeleteArchiveData(Database::Customer);
        end;

        if CustomerCategory.IsEmpty() then
            InsertDefaultCustomerCategory();

        //TODO:
        //SetDefaultCustomerCategoryForEveryCustomer();

    end;

    // Insert the GOLD, SILVER, BRONZE reward levels
    procedure InsertDefaultCustomerCategory();
    begin
        InsertCustomerCategory('TOP', 'Top Customer');
        InsertCustomerCategory('MEDIUM', 'Standard Customer');
        InsertCustomerCategory('BAD', 'Bad Customer');
    end;

    // Create and insert a reward level in the "Reward" table.
    procedure InsertCustomerCategory(ID : Code[30]; Description : Text[250]);
    var
        CustomerCategory : Record "Customer Category";
```

Here, in the `OnInstallAppPerCompany` trigger, we check the archived version. If it's the 1.0.0.0 version, we restore the data and remove the archived data. Then, we check the Customer Category table and, if it's empty, we initialize it with some default values.

Here is the complete AL code:

```
codeunit 50105 CustomerCategoryInstall
{
    Subtype = Install;
    trigger OnInstallAppPerCompany();
    var
        archivedVersion : Text;
        CustomerCategory : Record "Customer Category";
    begin
        archivedVersion := NavApp.GetArchiveVersion;
        if archivedVersion = '1.0.0.0' then begin
            NavApp.RestoreArchiveData(Database::"Customer Category");
            NavApp.RestoreArchiveData(Database::Customer);
            NavApp.DeleteArchiveData(Database::"Customer Category");
            NavApp.DeleteArchiveData(Database::Customer);
        end;
        if CustomerCategory.IsEmpty() then
            InsertDefaultCustomerCategory();
        //Here we could fill the Customer Category field for every
          Customer in the database with the default value
        //SetDefaultCustomerCategoryForEveryCustomer();
    end;

    // Insert the GOLD, SILVER, BRONZE reward levels
    procedure InsertDefaultCustomerCategory();
    begin
        InsertCustomerCategory('TOP', 'Top Customer');
        InsertCustomerCategory('MEDIUM', 'Standard Customer');
        InsertCustomerCategory('BAD', 'Bad Customer');
    end;

    // Create and insert a Customer Category record
    procedure InsertCustomerCategory(ID : Code[30]; Description :
    Text[250]);
    var
        CustomerCategory : Record "Customer Category";
    begin
        CustomerCategory.Init();
        CustomerCategory.No := ID;
        CustomerCategory.Description := Description;
        CustomerCategory.Insert();
    end;
}
```

When we need to upgrade an extension, we need to create an upgrade codeunit (a codeunit with a `SubType` property of `Upgrade`). An upgrade codeunit supports the following triggers:

- `OnCheckPreconditionsPerCompany()` and `OnCheckPreconditionsPerDatabase()`: Useful for checking that certain requirements are met before running the upgrade.
- `OnUpgradePerCompany()` and `OnUpgradePerDatabase()`: Used to perform the actual upgrade.
- `OnValidateUpgradePerCompany()` and `OnValidateUpgradePerDatabase()`: Used to check that the upgrade was successful.

As before, `PerCompany` triggers runs for each company in the database while `PerDatabase` triggers run once for the entire process.

This is an example of an `UpgradeCodeunit` for our previously-developed extension:

```al
codeunit 50106 CustomerCategoryUpgrade
{
    //IMPORTANT: Remember to increase the version number of the extension in the app.json file
    //Upgrade-NAVApp cmdlet

    Subtype = Upgrade;

    // "OnUpgradePerCompany" trigger is used to perform the actual upgrade.
    trigger OnUpgradePerCompany();
    var
        CustomerCategory : Record "Customer Category";

        // "ModuleInfo" is the current executing module.
        Module : ModuleInfo;
    begin
        // Get information about the current module.
        NavApp.GetCurrentModuleInfo(Module);

        // In the new version, the BAD class is upgraded to WARNING
        if Module.DataVersion.Major = 1 then begin
            IF CustomerCategory.Get('BAD') THEN BEGIN
                CustomerCategory.Rename('WARNING');
                CustomerCategory.Description := 'Warning Customer [UPG]';
                CustomerCategory.Modify();
            END;
        end;
    end;
}
```

Here, in the `OnUpgradePerCompany` trigger, we retrieve the current executing module information (`ModuleInfo`). Then, if the currently-running extension is version 1 (`Module.DataVersion.Major = 1`), we perform some upgrade operations on data (here we change the BAD customer category to `WARNING`).

Here is the complete AL code:

```
codeunit 50106 CustomerCategoryUpgrade
{
    Subtype = Upgrade;

    trigger OnUpgradePerCompany();
    var
        CustomerCategory : Record "Customer Category";
        Module : ModuleInfo;
    begin
        // Get information about the current module.
        NavApp.GetCurrentModuleInfo(Module);
        // In the new version, the BAD class is upgraded to WARNING
        if Module.DataVersion.Major = 1 then begin
            IF CustomerCategory.Get('BAD') THEN BEGIN
                CustomerCategory.Rename('WARNING');
                CustomerCategory.Description := 'Warning Customer [UPG]';
                CustomerCategory.Modify();
            END;
        end;
    end;
}
```

You can also check the dependencies' preconditions before updating your extension. Here a quick example of how to do that:

```
trigger OnCheckPreconditionsPerDatabase();
var
    DependentModuleInfo: ModuleInfo;
begin
    NavApp.GetModuleInfo('abcdegf5a-32ae-4d99-bb1c-81e02d123456',DependentModuleInfo);
    if DependentModuleInfo.DataVersion.Major < 3 then
        error('App %1 needs to be upgraded to version 3 first', DependentModuleInfo.Name)
end;
```

# Summary

In this chapter, we looked at how to implement an extension for Dynamics 365 Business Central and how to create all the types of objects available in the Extension model. You're now able to create your first extension and you're ready to deploy it on Dynamics 365 Business Central.

In Chapter 6, *Deploying Extensions*, we'll see how to debug your extension during the development phases and how to publish your extension to a Dynamics 365 Business Central production tenant.

# 6
# Deploying Extensions

In the previous chapter, we learned how to master AL language development and the core skills needed to code for extensions. In this chapter, we'll see how to deploy an extension in Dynamics 365 Business Central sandbox, production, and on-premises with Docker contained environment. The last section will also cover the basic principle of debugging extensions with some useful tips.

In this chapter, we will cover the following topics:

- What it means to deploy an extension, and the different types of extension deployment
- Impact of extension deployment at the database level
- Basics of extension debugging
- How to enable code analyzers

## What does extension deployment mean?

The extension deployment is made up of different phases, but roughly it means transforming the flat design-time written AL code into its equivalent runtime execution in the test, staging, or production environment. Deploying an extension can be done in four different ways:

- Automatically
- Semi-automatically
- Manually
- Through AppSource

The adoption of each of these depends on the technologies used and which environment type the extension is targeting: test or production, cloud-based or on-premises, custom-single-tenant or standard-multiple-tenant distribution.

# Automatic deployment

This is done through Visual Studio Code with the AL language enabled. It could be done directly through Dynamics 365 Business Central sandbox or in Docker contained sandbox staging environments.

> It cannot be done automatically in Dynamics 365 Business Central production tenants.

Deployment can be invoked in different ways, by:

- Pressing *F5*
- Running the command palette: `AL:Publish`
- Selecting from the menu bar: **Debug** | **Start Debugging**

When the AL language extension is enabled, the deployment command performs the following actions:

- Builds/rebuilds the extension package (same as doing *Ctrl* + *Shift* + *B* or command pallette `AL:Package`)

The AL compiler is triggered to parse the syntax for all the relevant files and then build the `.app` package. This operation output is rendered in the Visual Studio console window in the **OUTPUT** tab:

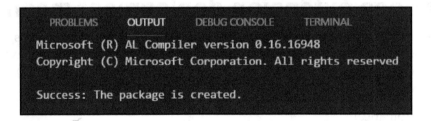

- Connects to the development sandbox instance: A connecting HTTP request is built and sent to an appropriate URL endpoint, based on parameters written in the `launch.json` file. This could be an online or on-premise, docker-contained, sandbox.

- Publishes the extension: When a connection is established with the development instance, the `.app` package is sent to the tenant database, ready to be available at runtime. No metadata changes are applied at this stage, only a basic validation against other extensions, such as if related dependencies are already published or if there are no duplicates, such as ID, name, or versioning.

- Installs the extension: This task triggers the extension metadata changes and executes the installation/upgrade code. If the extension is not already installed and if an Install Codeunit is deployed, the code written inside the Install Codeunit is triggered. This happens right after all the metadata changes and objects loaded at runtime.

From the connection authentication up to the end of the extension installation, the output result is typically displayed in the Visual Studio console window, in the **DEBUG CONSOLE** tab:

```
PROBLEMS    OUTPUT    DEBUG CONSOLE    TERMINAL
[2018-06-23 17:30:04.40] Authenticating...
[2018-06-23 17:30:05.55] Sending request to https://api.businesscentral.dynamics.com/v1.0/sandbox/dev/apps?SchemaUpdateMode=synchronize
[2018-06-23 17:30:11.04] Success: The package 'Default publisher_TESTDEPLOY_1.0.0.0.app' has been published to the server.
```

- Runs the development-sandbox instance hyperlink with store credentials

At this stage, the extension deployment is completed, and to test the effectiveness of the changes, based on `launch.json` parameters, Visual Studio Code invokes the Dynamics 365 Business Central sandbox URL.

Developers can then check in the web client the outcome of their customization. If something does not work as expected, they have to amend the offending code and when done, deploy the extension again as per typical develop-test cycle.

What counts most in the automatic deployment phase is where you are distributing the extension. This is reflected in the `launch.json` file and parameter settings.

The `launch.json` file contains an array of configurations. By default, only one configuration is created, but if you intend to automatically deploy the same application into different test environments, you could specify different configuration elements in the JSON array. Here is a parameter definition schema for the `launch.json` file:

| Setting | Mandatory | Example value | Remarks | Deployment type |
|---|---|---|---|---|
| type | Yes | .al | Fixed Value (required for Debugger). | All |
| request | Yes | Launch | Fixed Value (required for Debugger). | All |
| name | Yes | Dynamics 365 Business Central Sandbox MyCompany | Value should be able to define the environment to publish the extension to. | All |

| server | Yes | `http://serverinstance` | URL of your server. | Local on-premises |
|---|---|---|---|---|
| serverInstance | Yes | DynamicsNAV120 | Defines the server instance. | Local on-premises |
| authentication | Yes | AAD, UserPassword, Windows | Defines the server authentication method. | Local on-premises |
| startupObjectType | No | Page, Table | Which object type to open in the client, right after automatic deployment. | All |
| startupObjectId | No | 22 | ID of the object to open, right after automatic deployment. | All |
| schemaUpdateMode | No | Synchronize, Recreate | Synchronize is the default method and retains table data changes after publishing. Recreate will remove data every time the extension is published. | All |
| tenant | No | Default | In Multitenancy, specify which tenant to deploy the extension to. | All |

The following is a `launch.json` file sample for different configuration elements in a JSON array notation:

```json
{} launch.json ×
{
    "version": "0.2.0",
    "configurations": [
        {
            "type": "al",
            "request": "launch",
            "name": "Dynamics 365 Business Central Cloud Sandbox",
            "startupObjectId": 22,
            "startupObjectType": "Page"
        },
        {
            "type": "al",
            "request": "launch",
            "name": "On-Premise Local Dynamics 365 Business Central Docker Contained Sandbox",
            "server": "http://bcdocker",
            "serverInstance": "NAV",
            "authentication": "Windows"
        },
        {
            "type": "al",
            "request": "launch",
            "name": "On-Premise Azure VM hosted Dynamics 365 Business Central Docker Contained Sandbox",
            "server": "http://bcdocker.cloudapp.net",
            "serverInstance": "NAV",
            "authentication": "UserPassword"
        }
    ]
}
```

When downloading symbols or deploying an extension, the AL languge runtime will prompt you to choose which of the `launch.json` array elements will determine the connection parameters:

> Please choose the server:
>
> **Dynamics 365 Business Central Cloud Sandbox**
> Microsoft cloud sandbox
>
> **On-Premise Local Dynamics 365 Business Central Docker Contained Sandbox**
> http://bcdocker, NAV, tenant default
>
> **On-Premise Azure VM hosted Dynamics 365 Business Central Docker Contained Sandbox**
> http://bcdocker.cloudapp.net, NAV, tenant default

# Semi-automatic deployment

This could be done through a set of Windows PowerShell cmdlets (also known as PowerShell script). Currently, these Windows PowerShell cmdlets work against a Dynamics 365 Business Central Server service and are capable of differentiating between the publish phase and the installation phase.

Windows PowerShell scripts cannot be used with Dynamics 365 Business Central production or sandbox environments. They can only be used in on-premises sandbox environments, hence these can only be used with Docker-contained installations, hosted locally or deployed in Azure VMs.

Back in `Chapter 4`, *Creating Your Development Sandbox*, we learned how to create an Azure-hosted Dynamics 365 Business Central Docker-contained sandbox with a shortcut to the Docker-contained CSIDE, PowerShell ISE and NAVContainerHelper command prompts.

Roughly speaking, the automatic extension deployment through Visual Studio Code could be divided into different tasks using the appropriate cmdlets that, packed up in a script, might result in the very same final deployment outcome.

For this purpose, it is recommended to use the open source `NavContainerHelper` library. In the Azure VM, you might opt for the `NavContainerHelper` PowerShell prompt or directly use PowerShell ISE:

In the following example, we will use PowerShell ISE:

1. Run the PowerShell ISE as administrator in the Azure-hosted VM. This will come preloaded with the NavContainerHelper commandlet library.

Get familiar with the NavContainerHelper library. You can find more information about it at `https://blogs.msdn.microsoft.com/freddyk/tag/navcontainerhelper/`.

2. Run **Get-NavContainers** to find out which containers are deployed in this machine. This will return the name of the containers deployed in the AzureVM. Typically, there is only one deployed, called **navserver**, and this will be used to publish the app.
3. Publish the app by running the following statement where you specify the container name (navserver) and the path where to pick up the extension. the `SkipVerification` switch is used in this context because the app has not been signed with a certificate:

```
Publish-NavContainerApp -containerName navserver -appFile
C:\DEMO\TEST.app -skipVerification
```

The commandlet will:

- Copy the `.app` file from the specified folder in the container, if needed
- Open a Power Shell session inside the container and run Publish-NAVApp cmdlet against the contained database (`https://docs.microsoft.com/en-us/ powershell/module/microsoft.dynamics.nav.apps.management/publish- navapp?view=dynamicsnav-ps-2018`):

```
PS C:\demo> Publish-NavContainerApp -containerName navserver -appFile C:\DEMO\TEST.app -skipVerification
Copy C:\DEMO\TEST.app to container navserver (c:\run\TEST.app)
Welcome to the NAV Container PowerShell prompt

Publishing c:\run\TEST.app
App successfully published
```

4. You can then use the following code to synchronize the metadata content by running the Sync-NAVApp cmdlet against the contained database by specifying the container name. See, as follows, the official definition and usage for Sync-NAVApp: `https://docs.microsoft.com/en-us/powershell/module/ microsoft.dynamics.nav.apps.management/sync-navapp?view=dynamicsnav- ps-2018`.

```
Sync-NavContainerApp -containerName navserver -appName ALProject1
```

```
PS C:\demo> Sync-NavContainerApp -containerName navserver -appName ALProject1
Synchronizing c:\run\TEST.app on default
App successfully synchronized
```

5. Install the extension with the following code, by providing the container name and the app name:

```
Install-NavContainerApp -containerName navserver -appName ALProject1
```

```
PS C:\demo> Install-NavContainerApp -containerName navserver -appName ALProject1
Installing ALProject1 on default
App successfully installed
```

If you now run the docker-contained Windows client or connect to the docker-contained web client instance, you will see that the extension is appropriately deployed, and up and running:

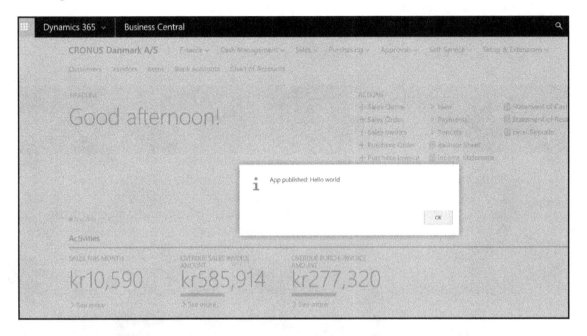

6. You can revert the extension deployment by uninstalling and unpublishing the app, using the following code, specifying container and app names:

```
UnInstall-NavContainerApp –containerName navserver –appName ALProject1
UnPublish-NavContainerApp-containerName navserver-appName ALProject1
```

```
PS C:\demo> UnInstall-NavContainerApp -containerName navserver -appName ALProject1
UnPublish-NavContainerApp -containerName navserver -appName ALProject1

Uninstalling ALProject1 from default
App successfully uninstalled
Unpublishing ALProject1

App successfully unpublished
```

Let's analyze what's happening at the database level in the publish, synchronize, and install deployment steps.

To verify every single deployment action, it's worth checking what is happening in every table when performing these actions. We will employ T-SQL queries to inspect the relevant tables and table changes that are involved in the extension deployment.

In the example that will follow, we will create a first extension and deploy it in a local Docker-contained Microsoft Dynamics 365 Business Central installation, and then we will also analyze what is happening when a second extension, dependent on the first one, is deployed.

To create the local Docker-Contained Micrsoft Dynamics 365 Business Central instance, as we learned in Chapter 4, *Creating Your Development Sandbox,* just run an elevated PowerShell ISE in your laptop and execute the following code:

```
#Install internet libraries (needs PowerShell 3.0 or higher and admin
privilege)
######################################################################
#####
 install-module navcontainerhelper -force
#Set local variables for license path and Docker image name to be used and
container name
######################################################################
#############
 $mylicense = 'C:\DOCKER\CSIDE\license2018.flf'
 $imageName = "microsoft/bcsandbox"
 $containerName = 'BCSANDBOX'
#Create a new container with Windows authentication
 ##################################################
 New-NavContainer -accept_eula `
                 -containerName $containerName `
                 -imageName $imageName `
                 -auth Windows `
                 -updateHosts `
                 -licenseFile $mylicense `
                 -doNotExportObjectsToText `
                 -includeCSide
```

You will be prompted to provide your Windows credentials. These will be used within the Docker-contained Microsoft Dynamics 365 Business Central sandbox instance to access windows client, web client and development environment. The scrip will generate 4 self-explaining shortcuts in your desktop:

- BCSANDBOX Command Prompt
- BCSANDBOX PowerShell Prompt

- BCSANDBOX Windows Client
- BCSANDBOX CSIDE

We will make use of some of these shortcuts later on. Let's create a couple of extensions, first.

1. Run Visual Studio Code from your laptop
2. Click on the **Extension** sidebar
3. In the **Extension** activity bar, search for AL Language and install it from marketplace
4. Reload Visual Studio Code, when prompted. See the following screenshot, what you might expect after reloading:

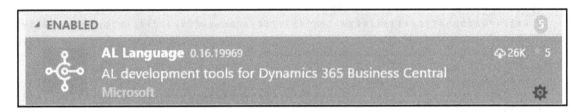

If you are developing IPs for both Microsoft Dynamics NAV 2018 and Microsoft Dynamics 365 Business Central, you must use the appropriate AL language extension version, targeted for a specific platform. It is recommended to opt for keeping enabled for workspace only the AL language extension for the supported platform and click on **Disable** (workspace) the other AL language(s) extensions.

5. Create a new extension from scratch by running the command pallette (*Ctrl + Shift + P*) and select AL: GO!
6. Give a name to your extension folder (such as FIRSTEXTENSION) when prompted and choose to connect to local server, which is the second option offered.
7. Change the launch.json file to connect to your on-premise Docker-contained Microsoft Dynamics 365 Business Central installation. Here is an example:

```json
1  {
2      "version": "0.2.0",
3      "configurations": [
4          {
5              "type": "al",
6              "request": "launch",
7              "name": "Your own server",
8              "server": "http://BCSANDBOX",
9              "serverInstance": "NAV",
10             "authentication": "Windows",
11             "startupObjectId": 22,
12             "startupObjectType": "Page"
13         }
14     ]
15 }
```

8. Change the `app.json` file in the following way:

```json
1  {
2      "id": "84a521ce-2c19-4857-9811-7e6a015b9b52",
3      "name": "FIRST EXTENSION",
4      "publisher": "Tacconi Inc.",
5      "brief": "",
6      "description": "",
7      "version": "1.0.0.0",
8      "privacyStatement": "",
9      "EULA": "",
10     "help": "",
11     "url": "",
12     "logo": "",
13     "capabilities": [],
14     "dependencies": [],
15     "screenshots": [],
16     "platform": "12.0.0.0",
17     "application": "12.0.0.0",
18     "idRange": {
19         "from": 50100,
20         "to": 50149
21     }
22 }
```

9. Download Symbols from the Microsoft Dynamics 365 Business Central database: run the command pallette (*Ctrl + Shift + P*) and select **AL: Download symbols**.

10. Remove the automatically created `HelloWorld.al` file and create two new files, named as follows and with the code in the screenshots:

`PAGEEXT.50101.CustomerListExt.al:`

```
0 references
pageextension 50100 CustomerListExt extends "Customer List"
{
    trigger OnOpenPage();
    begin
        Message('Flower and Fruit App published');
    end;
}
```

`TABLE.50100.Flower.al:`

```
0 references
table 50100 Flower
{
    DataClassification = ToBeClassified;

    fields
    {
        1 reference
        field(1;MyField;Integer)
        {
            DataClassification = ToBeClassified;
        }
        0 references
        field(2;Name;Code[30])
        {
            DataClassification = ToBeClassified;
        }
        0 references
        field(3;Description;Text[50])
        {
            DataClassification = ToBeClassified;
        }
    }

    keys
    {
        - reference
        key(PK;MyField)
        {
            Clustered = true;
        }
    }
}
```

11. Build the package (*Ctrl + Shift + B*)
12. Publish the first extension in the database by pressing *F5*

Fair enough. We have now a fully working extension deployed in our Microsoft Dynamics 365 Business Central database. Now it is time to create a second extension that is dependent on the first extension:

1. Create a new extension from scratch by running the Command Palette (*Ctrl + Shift + P*) and select **AL!GO**

2. Give a name to your extension folder (such as `ALSecondExtension`) when prompted and choose to connect to local server, which is the second option offered.

3. Change the `launch.json` file to connect to your On-Premise Dynamics NAV 2018 installation, as in previous example.

4. Change the `app.json` file in the following way:

```
{
    "id": "6106f7a9-36bf-4a4c-8480-f2198b711101",
    "name": "SECOND EXTENSION",
    "publisher": "Tacconi Inc.",
    "brief": "",
    "description": "",
    "version": "1.0.0.0",
    "privacyStatement": "",
    "EULA": "",
    "help": "",
    "url": "",
    "logo": "",
    "capabilities": [],
    "dependencies": [
        {
            "appId" : "84a521ce-2c19-4857-9811-7e6a015b9b52",
            "name": "FIRST EXTENSION",
            "publisher": "Tacconi Inc.",
            "version": "1.0.0.0"
        }
    ],
    "screenshots": [],
    "platform": "12.0.0.0",
    "application": "12.0.0.0",
    "idRange": {
        "from": 50100,
        "to": 50149
    }
}
```

5. Download Symbols from the Microsoft Dynamics 365 Business Central database: use the command palette (*Ctrl* + *Shift* + *P*) and select **Download Symbols**.

 You might notice that you now have three symbols file: `Application`, `System`, and `FIRST EXTENSION`. This happens because the second extension has been declared as dependant on the first one.

> ◢ .alpackages
> ≣ Microsoft_Application_12.3.23828.0.app
> ≣ Microsoft_System_12.0.12928.0.app
> ≣ Tacconi Inc._FIRST EXTENSION_1.0.0.0.app

6. Remove the `HelloWorld.al` file and create three files, named as follow and with the code in the screenshots:

`TABLE.50101.Fruit:`

```
0 references
table 50101 Fruit|
{
    DataClassification = ToBeClassified;

    fields
    {
        1 reference
        field(1;MyField;Integer)
        {
            DataClassification = ToBeClassified;
        }
        0 references
        field(2;Name;Code[30])
        {
            DataClassification = ToBeClassified;
        }
        0 references
        field(3;Description;Text[50])
        {
            DataClassification = ToBeClassified;
        }
    }

    keys
    {
        - reference
        key(PK;MyField)
        {
            Clustered = true;
        }
    }
}
```

PAGE.50100.FlowerList.al:

```al
0 references
page 50100 "Flower List"
{
    PageType = List;
    SourceTable = Flower;

    layout
    {
        0 references
        area(content)
        {
            0 references
            repeater(Group)
            {
                0 references
                field(Name;Name)
                {
                    ApplicationArea=All;
                }
                0 references
                field(Description;Description)
                {
                    ApplicationArea=All;
                }
            }
        }
    }
}
```

`PAGE.50101.FlowerCard.al`:

```
0 references
page 50101 "Flower Card"
{
    PageType = Card;
    SourceTable = Flower;

    layout
    {
        0 references
        area(content)
        {
            0 references
            group(GroupName)
            {
                0 references
                field(Name;Name)
                {
                    ApplicationArea=All;
                }
                0 references
                field(Description;Description)
                {
                    ApplicationArea=All;
                }
            }
        }
    }
}
```

7. Build the package (*Ctrl + Shift + B*).
8. Do not deploy the extension, instead copy and rename the `.app` package generated to `C:\TEMP\SecondExtension.app`.

It's time now to experiment and analyze the changes in the metadata structure when deploying an extension.

# Publishing

Run an elevated PowerShell ISE and execute the contained publish cmdlet by providing the container name and the extension path:

```
Publish-NAVContainerApp -containerName BCSANDBOX -appFile
"C:\TEMP\SecondExtension.app" -skipVerification
```

The publish action performs the following tasks:

- Uploads the `.app` file through Microsoft Dynamics 365 Business Central Server service
- Unpacks the `.app` content in memory
- Populates several tables in the application database based on the `.app` content

At the end of this action:

- No changes are applied to the metadata structure
- No **user experience** (**UX**) or business logic changes are applied

This process simply stores the extension content inside the application database, ready to be synchronized (distributed) in every tenant for a subsequent potential installation on demand.

Run SQL Server Management Studio (SSMS) and connect to the SQL Server Express instance inside the Docker container (`BCSANDBOX\SQLEXPRESS`) using your Windows credentials. Click on **New Query** (*Ctrl + N*), and paste the following T-SQL scripts. Generate a new query for each script.

**SqlScript1**: return the current records (status) of the `NAV App` tables:

```
--Select the Database
use [FinancialsW1]
go
--NAV APP Tables: relates each other by NAV APP ID
declare @Appid uniqueidentifier
select @Appid = '6106f7a9-36bf-4a4c-8480-f2198b711101' --Change this value
with "id" field value in the App.json file
SELECT * FROM [dbo].[NAV App] WHERE ID=@Appid
SELECT * FROM [dbo].[NAV App Data Archive] WHERE [App ID]=@Appid
SELECT * FROM [dbo].[NAV App Installed App] WHERE [App ID]=@Appid
SELECT * FROM [dbo].[NAV App Tenant Add-In] WHERE [App ID]=@Appid
SELECT * FROM [dbo].[NAV App Published App] WHERE [App ID]=@Appid
```

Here are the results:

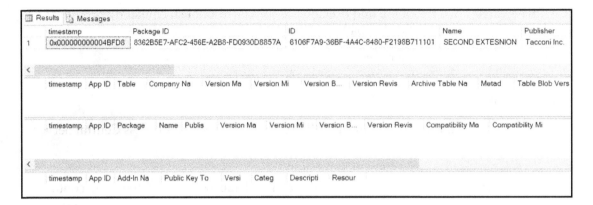

The record is written in the `NAV App` table, which stores the `.app` file in the `Blob` field and writes several fields based on the `app.json` file. The `Package ID` field is also assigned to determine relationships with other tables involved in future deployment phases.

If your extension contains a logo (an image), this is stored as a blob field in the `Media` table. You can retrieve the record by running this query:

```
select * from dbo.Media
WHERE ID = '0DD96B18-E178-4BB0-A111-0163F3F113BA' -- Change this value with
"Logo" field value in [NAV APP] table
```

**SqlScript2**: Return the current records (status) of the NAV App package content-related tables. These have a relationship with the NAV App table through the Package ID field:

```
--Select the Database
use [FinancialsW1]
go

--NAV APP Package Tables: related to NAV App table by PACKAGE ID
declare @xAppid uniqueidentifier
select @xAppid = '6106f7a9-36bf-4a4c-8480-f2198b711101' --Change this value
with "id" field value in the App.json file
declare @PackageID uniqueidentifier
select @PackageID = (SELECT [Package ID] FROM [dbo].[NAV App] WHERE
ID=@xAppid)

SELECT * FROM [dbo].[NAV App Capabilities] WHERE [Package ID]=@PackageID
SELECT * FROM [dbo].[NAV App Dependencies] WHERE [Package ID]=@PackageID
```

```
SELECT * FROM [dbo].[NAV App Object Metadata] WHERE [App Package
ID]=@PackageID
SELECT * FROM [dbo].[NAV App Object Prerequisites] WHERE [Package
ID]=@PackageID
SELECT * FROM [dbo].[NAV App Resource] WHERE [Package ID]=@PackageID
SELECT * FROM [dbo].[NAV App Tenant App] WHERE [App Package ID]=@PackageID
SELECT * FROM [dbo].[NAV App Publish Reference] WHERE [App Package
ID]=@PackageID
```

Here are the results:

| timestamp | Package | Capability ID | | | | | | | | |
|---|---|---|---|---|---|---|---|---|---|---|

| | timestamp | Package ID | ID | | | Name | Publisher | Version Ma | Version Mi | Version B... |
|---|---|---|---|---|---|---|---|---|---|---|
| 1 | 0x000000000004BFDB | 8362B5E7-AFC2-456E-A2B8-FD0930D8857A | 84A521CE-2C19-4857-9811-7E6A015B9B52 | | | FIRST EXTENSION | Tacconi Inc. | 1 | 0 | 0 |

| | timestamp | App Package ID | Object Ty | Object | Metadata For | Metadata | | | | User Code |
|---|---|---|---|---|---|---|---|---|---|---|
| 1 | 0x000000000004BFE2 | 8362B5E7-AFC2-456E-A2B8-FD0930D8857A | 1 | 50101 | 0 | 0x02457D5BD5956D6F9B3010C7DF4FDA77B0FC9E059234A51... | | | | 0x02457D5BC |
| 2 | 0x000000000004BFE8 | 8362B5E7-AFC2-456E-A2B8-FD0930D8857A | 8 | 50100 | 0 | 0x02457D5BC556DB6EDB38107D5F60FF41D03E2BBA58BEC2... | | | | 0x02457D5BC |
| 3 | 0x000000000004BFDE | 8362B5E7-AFC2-456E-A2B8-FD0930D8857A | 8 | 50101 | 0 | 0x02457D5BC5566D6FDB3610FE3E60FF41E03E2B92FC26C5B... | | | | 0x02457D5BC |

| timestamp | Package | Ty | ID | | | | |
|---|---|---|---|---|---|---|---|

| | timestamp | Package ID | Ty | Name | Content | |
|---|---|---|---|---|---|---|
| 1 | 0x000000000004BFDC | 8362B5E7-AFC2-456E-A2B8-FD0930D8857A | 1 | metadata | 0x02457D5BABE6E55250500A28CA4FCBCC49F54D2D494C49 | |

| timestamp | Tenant | App Package | | |
|---|---|---|---|---|

One record is inserted in the NAV App Dependencies table with reference to the FIRST EXTENSION ID and definition. You will find more records if there are more dependencies defined in the app.json file for the published extension.

The most important part in this context is NAV App Object Metadata, which stores three records. These are the objects defined in the extension, in this case we have 1 table object (Object Type 1) with ID 50101 and two page objects (Object Type 8) with ID 50100 and 50101. The Metadata and User Code fields store, respectively, the metadata structure (XML format) and converted C# code (.cs format) for the extension object.

**SqlScript3**: Returns the current records (status) of the NAV App Schema related tables. These have a relationship with the NAV App table through the ID field:

```
--Select the Database
use [FinancialsW1]
go

--NAV APP Schema Tables: related to NAV App table by ID
declare @id uniqueidentifier
select @id = '6106f7a9-36bf-4a4c-8480-f2198b711101' --Change this value
with "id" field value in the App.json file

SELECT * FROM [dbo].[$ndo$navappschemasnapshot] WHERE appid = @id
```

```
SELECT * FROM [dbo].[$ndo$navappschematracking] WHERE appid = @id
SELECT * FROM [dbo].[$ndo$navappuninstalledapp] WHERE appid = @id
```

What are the results?

There are no changes. This is because the `Publish` action does not generate any action on metadata or the database schema.

## Syncronizing

In the elevated PowerShell ISE Command Prompt, type:

```
Sync-NAVContainerApp -containerName BCSANDBOX -tenant default -appName
"SECOND EXTENSION"
```

Now execute all three SQL scripts and check what has changed during the synchronization phase:

- **SqlScript1**: No changes
- **SqlScript2**: No changes
- **SqlScript3**: You will notice that the `navappschemasnapshot` table has been populated with the Table 50101 Fruit record, and the `navappschematracking` table has one record to track schema changes for the extension:

The *synchronize* action instructs the system to create the database structure for the application to track schema changes in the relevant tenant. In this specific case, with legacy mode, the database acts like a single tenant, named default, that now is ready for the installation on demand.

## Installing

In the elevated PowerShell ISE Command Prompt, type the following:

```
Install-NAVApp -ServerInstance DynamicsNAV110 -Name "SECOND EXTENSION"
```

Execute all three SQL scripts and check what has changed during the installation phase:

- **SqlScript1**: A new record is created in the `Nav App Installed App` table. Roughly, this is s a copy of the NAV App record. All the records in this table correspond to the equivalent extensions installed that changed the metadata and business rules according to what they had been developed for:

- **SqlScript2**: A new record for the default tenant is created in the NAV App Tenant App table to keep track of a specific package ID that belongs to a NAV App ID:

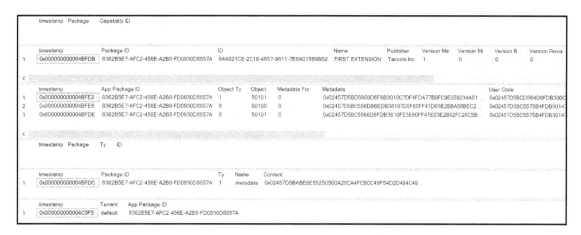

A new record for NAV App Tenant APP table to keep track of sepecific ID

- **SqlScript3**: No changes

Looking deeper at the table structure, you could see that a new table has been created during the installation process composed by the table name, as defined in the table object, and the app ID:

The installation action instructs the Microsoft Dynamics 365 Business Central Server service to apply database structure changes in order to align with the current metadata provided with the extension object. Moreover, the objects that pertain to the same extensions are loaded into server memory, and users can observe UX and business-process changes. This is the most delicate of all three deployment phases.

> You might want to use these three scripts when testing the deployment of your own extension and observe the impact of publishing, synchronizing, and installing your private IP at the database level. This could be fruitful during deployment-troubleshooting.

# Manual deployment

This is the easiest and most common deployment type. It can be done in all the environment types and is the only allowed deployment method for production tenants. It just implies that you have a finished extension in the form of the `.app` file.

To manually deploy an extension in production:

1. With a web browser, connect to your production Microsoft Dynamics 365 Business Central instance and select whatever company you like.

> Currently, the extension deployment is per-tenant-based and not per-company-based. If you need to have a specific feature enabled per-company, the extension must have some code that would inhibit the usage in a custom company setup. Nevertheless, the extension objects always remain installed per-tenant.

2. Click on the **Setup & Extensions** menu and then select **Extensions**:

Setup & Extensions ⌄

This menu is typically related to Role Center, where the user is logged in. Business Manager is one of the Role Centers packed up with this menu.

3. From the **Extensions** menu bar, choose **Manage** and select **Upload Extension**:

4. Browse to the folder where you have your extension (`.app`) file to upload and install:

5. The upload (publish) and install operations are asynchronous—check the deployment status periodically until the installation has ended. As mentioned previously, the installation deployment phase is the most delicate one and it might take some time depending on the extension type and its complexity. To check the deployment status, in the **Extensions** menu, select **Manage|Deployment Status**. This will show all deployment statuses in a list format, you can select your record and check the card to see whether it is still in progress or whether there are any issues during deployment:

# AL debugger

The last part of this chapter deals with a developer's bread and butter (whatever language they are specialized in): the debugger.

Visual Studio Code has built-in debugging support for Node.js runtime, and is capable of debugging JavaScript, JavaScript-derived, and TypeScript languages. All other language extensions might implement their own debugger based on the Visual Studio Code debugger extension API. If you want to learn more about the Visual Studio Code debugger, check out `https://code.visualstudio.com/docs/editor/debugging`.

AL language debugger comes integrated with the AL language extension. Its output is surfaced on the built-in Visual Studio Code debugger View. it can be enabled in different ways from Visual Studio Code:

- Using the shortcut, *F5* (start with debugging)
- From the Palette command (*Ctrl + Shift + P*), select **AL!Publish**
- From the menu bar, choose **Start | Start Debugging**

It's good to start with a simple hands-on example with AL debugger. In the following example, we have been asked to enable the Work Description calculated field (BLOB field) in the Sales Invoice document:

1. Run Visual Studio Code with AL Language for Dynamics 365 Business Central, which is already installed
2. Create a new HelloWorld sample (AL!GO)
3. Change `launch.json` to start with page `9301` (Sales Invoice list):

```
"startupObjectId": 9301,
"startupObjectType": "Page"
```

4. Change the `app.json` file like the following, by adding two extra parameters, showMyCode and `target`:

```json
{
  "id": "de7687ce-cb19-41a8-b225-4c91d183f1f4",
  "name": "TESTWORKDESC",
  "publisher": "DTACCONI",
  "brief": "",
  "description": "",
  "version": "1.0.0.0",
  "privacyStatement": "",
  "EULA": "",
  "help": "",
  "url": "",
  "logo": "",
  "capabilities": [],
  "dependencies": [],
  "screenshots": [],
  "platform": "12.0.0.0",
  "application": "12.0.0.0",
  "target": "Extension",
  "showMyCode": true,
  "idRange": {
    "from": 50100,
    "to": 50149
  }
}
```

The `showMyCode` Boolean parameter is used to protect private **intellectual property** (**IP**) and determines whether:

- The code could also be extracted where deployed by selecting the extension in the extension list and choosing **Download Source**:

- The code could be shown while debugging or using code coverage

The `target` parameter enables AL language to detect allowed statements, syntaxes, and data types based on different extension target types. These could be:

- **Extension:** Default value. To be used with Dynamics 365 Business Central.
- **Internal:** To be used with Dynamics NAV 2018 On-Premises. It allows for a less restricted syntax and data type usage (for example, the dotnet data type is only allowed when the target is internal, both in the extension and in the service configuration file).
- **Personalization:** Set when you save extensions using the In-Client designer. It does not cover or allow any table structure changes, only UX personalization artifacts, typically PageExtension objects.
- **Solution:** Currently not used. Reserved for future implementation, probably AppSource related.

5. Download symbols.

6. Rename `HelloWorld.al` as `PAGEEXT.50100.SalesInvoice.al`.

7. Change the code internally as per the following:

```
0 references
pageextension 50100 PageExtension50100 extends "Sales Invoice"
{
    layout
    {
        addafter("Status")
        {
            0 references
            field("EXT Your Reference";"Your Reference")
            {
                ApplicationArea=All;
            }
            0 references
            group("Wrkedscription")
            {

                CaptionML=ENU='Work Description',DAN='Work Description';

                0 references
                field("EXTWorkDescription";EXTWorkDescription)
                {
                    ApplicationArea=All;
                    ShowCaption=false;
                    MultiLine=true;
                    Importance=Promoted;

                    trigger OnValidate()
                    begin
                        SetWorkDescription(EXTWorkDescription);
                    end;
                }
            }
        }
    }

    trigger OnAfterGetRecord()
    begin
        EXTWorkDescription := GetWorkDescription();
    end;

    var
        3 references
        EXTWorkDescription: Text;

}
```

8. Add a Breakpoint into line 34. You can add a breakpoint:
   - By pressing *F9*
   - From the menu bar, select **Debug | Toggle Breakpoint**:

```
32      trigger OnAfterGetRecord()
33      begin
● 34    EXTWorkDescription := GetWorkDescription();
35      end;
36
```

9. Build the Extension (*Ctrl + Shift + B*)
10. Run with Debugging (*F5*)

NOTE: The Debug Console is activated

11. When the Sales Invoice list pops up in your browser, choose whatever Sales Invoice you like. This will open the Sales Invoice page and hit the OnAfterGetRecord trigger and our breakpoint.

AL debugger will be activated and Visual Studio Code will be presented in front of you in all the majesty of its debugger View. The status bar turns to orange, signaling it's in debug mode:

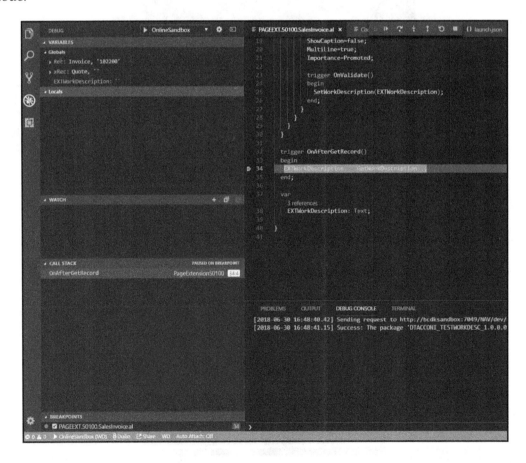

The debugger View includes four different sections: **Debug Activity** Pane with several tiled sub panes, **Debug Console**, **Code** Pane, and **Debug Activity** Buttons.

The **VARIABLES** tile displays the Global and Local variables for the specific call stack. You might want to expand or collapse global elements from the current example to check their values.

Clicking on the other tiles (such as **WATCH** and **CALL STACK**) will collapse them to give you a better overview of VARIABLES' content.

When AL debugger is activated, you could choose to take different debug actions manually or using buttons:

Practice with all the buttons; inspect how Step Over, Into, and Out influence the debugger Activity Pane (**VARIABLE** and **CALL STACK**), and press Stop when finished.

# AL CodeCop

**CodeCop** is a very interesting new addition for AL developers. it is a software artifact that checks, like a cop at the corner of the streets, if the code written respects specific rules (coding rules). This concept never existed in the old CSIDE and C/AL developers just keep their own rules in mind without anything specific to check whether these are applied.

You can find a basic reference for AL CodeCops at `https://docs.`
`microsoft.com/en-us/dynamics365/business-central/dev-itpro/`
`developer/devenv-using-code-analysis-tool.`

There are different type of Codecops, depending on the deployment type. These are used to bust specific unwanted semantic code and make the developer's coding more restricted and less open to fantasy or fancy solution, hard to check and maintain even by smart developers, and, overall, deviating from the standard Microsoft Development best practice.

Also called Diagnostic Descriptors or Code Analysis Rules there are currently four Codecops. See the following definitions and usage references:

- **CodeCop**: Enforces the official AL Coding Guidelines. It is useful for every kind of deployment, together with other, more specific, diagnostic descriptors.
- **PerTenantExtensionCop**: Enforces rules that must be respected by extensions meant to be installed for individual tenants.
- **AppSourceCop**: Enforces rules that must be respected by extension-development targeted for the AppSource marketplace.
- **UiCop**: Enforces rules that must be respected by extension-development targeted for Web-Client development.

CodeCops could be enabled by changing User or Workspace settings, depending on whether code analysis has to be performed on every extension development (User Settings) or per single extension development (workspace settings). These settings can be shown with different shortcuts:

- By pressing *Ctrl* + COMMA
- From the menu bar, **File** | **Preferences** | **Settings**
- Via the command palette (*Ctrl* + *Shift* + *P*), search for settings and choose **Preferences: Open Workspace Settings**:

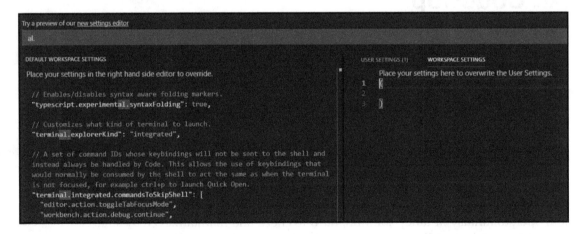

In the left pane, you can see the default values, while on the right pane, you can change or add entries for the very specific feature in the relevant tab: User or Workspace.

To enable Codecops, you have to declare `al.enableCodeAnalysis` as `true`. This will enable ALL the code descriptors. If you want to specify only some of them, you have to specify them in a JSON array notation with the `al.codeAnalyzers` parameter. Here is a simple example:

```
USER SETTINGS      WORKSPACE SETTINGS
        Place your settings here to overwrite the User Settings.
1    {
2          "al.enableCodeAnalysis": true,
3          "al.codeAnalyzers": [
4              "${CodeCop}",
5              "${PerTenantExtensionCop}"
6          ]
7    }
```

From now on, you might receive more error and warning messages, which will help you keep the code development more consistent, robust, and adhere to coding best practice. Just to give you an example, if the extension has been defined to target on-premises development (`"target": "Internal"`) and the workspace settings are defined to enable `CodeCop` and `PerTenantExtensionCop`, you cannot build the extension since an error is thrown:

```
error PTE0005: App.json 'target' property must not be set to 'Internal'.
Error: The package could not be created.
```

This happens because `PerTenantExtensionCop` is expecting to have target field to be set to *Extension* instead of *Internal*, hence it prevents you from building the `.app` file until you select the appropriate CodeCops or change the target parameter in `app.json`.

If you would like to extend Codecops, you could create your own rulesets. Rulesets are intended only to change the severity of diagnostics generated by existing Codecops. You could then decide to bypass certain warnings or to turn a warning into an error depending on your own company coding rules.

To learn more about rulesets, visit the following URL: `https://docs.microsoft.com/en-us/dynamics365/business-central/dev-itpro/developer/devenv-using-code-analysis-tool-with-rule-set`.

# Summary

In this chapter, we learned about the various options for deploying an extension targeted for Microsoft Dynamics 365 Business Central cloud sandbox or the on-premises Docker contained environment. We also covered the publish and install tasks related to extension deployment and the changes that happen inside the database.

In Chapter 7, *Integration and Serverless Processing*, we'll learn how to integrate external applications with Microsoft Dynamics 365 Business Central and how to build serverless business processes for Microsoft Dynamics 365 Business Central by using different Azure Services.

# Integration and Serverless Processing

In Chapter 6, *Deploying Extensions*, we saw how to deploy an extension to Dynamics 365 Business Central (sandbox or production environments) and how to debug our deployed code.

In this chapter, we'll see how we can integrate Dynamics 365 Business Central with external applications and how we can use some Azure-powered services in order to create serverless business processes. Here, you will learn the following:

- How to integrate with Dynamics 365 Business Central by using APIs and web services
- How to use Azure Functions and .NET code with Dynamics 365 Business Central
- How to interact with Microsoft Flow and Microsoft PowerApps to build serverless workflows

# Dynamics 365 Business Central web services

When talking about integrating Dynamics 365 Business Central with external applications in a service-oriented way, we have essentially two main roads: use SOAP and OData web services, or use REST APIs.

To publish a NAV entity as a SOAP web service, you have to go to the web service page in Dynamics 365 Business Central. For this sample, we want to create a web service to access the Item entity, so we create a new record by inserting the following values:

- **OBJECT TYPE:** Page
- **OBJECT ID:** 30
- **SERVICE NAME:** Item
- **PUBLISHED:** true

Dynamics 365 Business Central automatically gives you the URLs for the OData and SOAP endpoints:

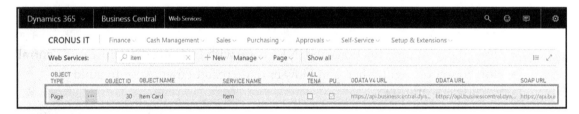

Now, you can access your published web service from an external application able to use SOAP web services.

To create a web service client, open Visual Studio and create a new Console application project (here called D365BCWebServiceClient). Now, right-click on your project and select **Add a Service Reference**.

In the **Address** box, enter the SOAP URL from your published web service, click **GO**, and enter a name for your web service instance (here it's D365BCItemService):

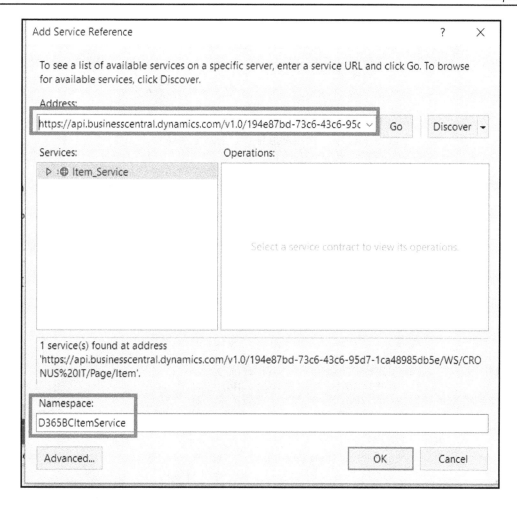

Click **OK** and Visual Studio will create the proxy class for your web service.

As an example of usage, in the `Main` function of our Console application, we create an instance of the web service and we retrieve the items by applying a filter.

The C# code is as follows:

```
using System;
using System.Collections.Generic;
using System.Linq;
using System.Net;
using System.ServiceModel;
using System.Text;
using System.Threading.Tasks;
```

```
using D365BCWebServiceClient.D365BCItemService;

namespace D365BCWebServiceClient
{
    class Program
    {
        static void Main(string[] args)
        {
            string WSKey = "YOURWEBSERVICEACCESSKEY";
            string WSURL =
        "https://api.businesscentral.dynamics.com/v1.0/194e87bd-
            73c6-43c6-95d7-1ca48985db5e/WS/CRONUS%20IT/Page/Item";
            //Create an instance of the D365BC SOAP WS
            BasicHttpBinding binding = new BasicHttpBinding();
            //Set HTTPS usage
            binding.Security.Mode = BasicHttpSecurityMode.Transport;
            binding.Security.Transport.ClientCredentialType =
            HttpClientCredentialType.Basic;
            D365BCItemService.Item_PortClient ws = new
            Item_PortClient(binding, new EndpointAddress(WSURL));
            ws.ClientCredentials.UserName.UserName = "sdemiliani";
            ws.ClientCredentials.UserName.Password = WSKey;
            //Creating the filters for retrieving the records
            List<Item_Filter> filters = new List<Item_Filter>();
            Item_Filter filter = new Item_Filter();
            filter.Field = Item_Fields.No;
            filter.Criteria = "1*";
            filters.Add(filter);
            try
            {
                foreach (Item item in
                ws.ReadMultiple(filters.ToArray(), "", 0))
                {
                    Console.WriteLine("No: {0} Name: {1}", item.No,
                    item.Description);
                }
            }
            catch (Exception ex)
            {
                Console.WriteLine("Error retrieving Items: {0}
                InnerException: {1}", ex.Message,
                ex.InnerException);
            }
            Console.ReadKey();
        }
    }
}
```

Obviously, you can also insert a record by using the `Create` or `CreateMultiple` methods, or update records by using the `Update` or `UpdateMultiple` methods.

To access Dynamics 365 Business Central web services, here we've used *basic authentication*. For that, you need to call a web service by passing your username and your generated web service access key as a password:

From Visual Studio, you can also add a reference to a SOAP web service from Dynamics 365 Business Central as an old-style .NET web service by going to **Add** | **Service Reference** | **Advanced** | **Add Web Reference**.

Here is a quick C# sample that uses the published `Customer Card` to insert a `Customer` into Business Central from a Console application as a SOAP .NET web service:

```
static void Main(string[] args)
        {
         string WSKey = "YOURWEBSERVICEACCESSKEY";
            //Create an instance of the D365BC SOAP WS
            Customer_Service ws = new Customer_Service();
            ws.Url =
            "https://api.businesscentral.dynamics.com/v1.0/194e87bd-
             73c6-43c6-95d7-1ca48985db5e/WS/CRONUS%20IT/Page/Customer";
            //Handling authentication
            System.Net.CredentialCache myCredentials = new
            System.Net.CredentialCache();
            NetworkCredential netCred = new
            NetworkCredential("sdemiliani", WSKey);
            myCredentials.Add(new Uri(ws.Url), "Basic", netCred);
            ws.Credentials = myCredentials;
            //Create the Customer record
            Customer customer = new Customer();
            customer.Name = "SOAP Customer";
```

```
customer.Address = "Viale Kennedy 87, Novara";
customer.Country_Region_Code = "IT";
customer.Blocked = Blocked.All;
try
{
    //Start the Create method
    ws.Create(ref customer);
    Console.WriteLine("Customer {0} created successfully.",
    customer.No);
}
catch (Exception ex)
{
    Console.WriteLine("Customer creation error: {0}
    InnerException: {1}", ex.Message, ex.InnerException);
}
}
```

When invoked, the customer record is created in Dynamics 365 Business Central:

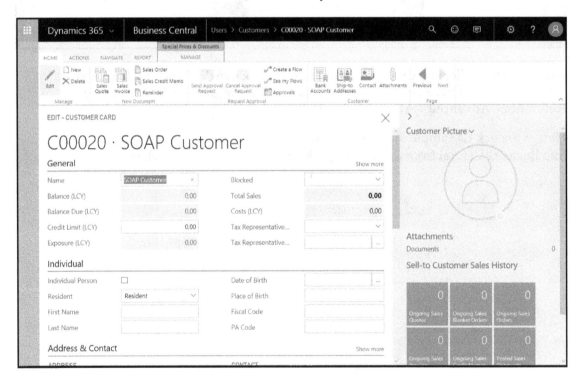

# Dynamics 365 Business Central REST APIs

At the time of writing, Dynamics 365 Business Central offers 44 standard APIs available for integration with external applications.

REST APIs permit you to create any type of application in any code language that interacts with Dynamics 365 Business Central by using HTTP **CRUD** operations (**create, retrieve, update, delete**).

To start using the APIs, you need to authenticate through Dynamics 365 Business Central. There are essentially two ways to authenticate:

- **Basic authentication**: Log in to Dynamics 365 Business Central, select the Users page, select the user you want to use, click on the Web Service Access Key field, and generate a key. The generated key will be the password that you have to use for authentication, together with your username. The API endpoint to use is the following: https://api.businesscentral.dynamics.com/v1.0/ <yourtenantID>/api/beta.

- **Azure Active Directory (AAD) authentication**: This is what should be used in a production environment. You need to sign in to Azure Portal in order to register Dynamics 365 Business Central as an app in your Azure Active Directory. More details can be found at https://docs.microsoft.com/en-us/dynamics365/ business-central/dev-itpro/developer/devenv-develop-connect- apps#setting-up-azure-active-directory-(aad)-based-authentication.

To use the APIs, you can simply send the GET, POST, PUT, DELETE, and PATCH HTTP commands by using the API endpoint and the proper authentication:

- GET r is used to retrieve a resource without modifying its state
- POST is used to create a new resource
- PUT is used to update existing resources (complete record update)
- DELETE is used to delete resources
- PATCH is used to perform a partial update on a resource (this is the main difference compared to PUT)

Here, we're using the Postman tool to create REST calls to Dynamics 365 Business Central APIs. We're using Basic authentication (username and web service access key).

In the first call, we send a GET call to retrieve the companies for our Dynamics 365 Business Central tenant (the GUID you can see in the URL is our tenant ID): `https://api.businesscentral.dynamics.com/v1.0/194e87bd-73c6-43c6-95d7-1ca48985db5e/api/beta/companies`.

This is the response obtained:

As you can see from the response, every record has its proper ID (a GUID) that we can use to retrieve specific information about that record. For example, if we want to retrieve information about a specific company (such as CRONUS IT), we have to send a GET call to the following URL (passing the company ID to retrieve): `https://api.businesscentral.dynamics.com/v1.0/194e87bd-73c6-43c6-95d7-1ca48985db5e/api/beta/companies(80d28ea6-02a3-4ec3-98f7-936c2000c7b3)`.

Now, the response is the following:

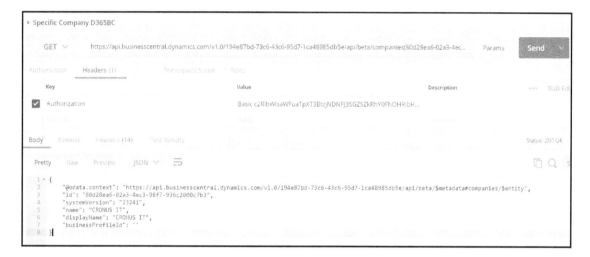

If now we want to retrieve all customers for a specific company (for example, CRONUS IT) we can send a GET call to the following URL: `https://api.businesscentral.dynamics.com/v1.0/194e87bd-73c6-43c6-95d7-1ca48985db5e/api/beta/companies(80d28ea6-02a3-4ec3-98f7-936c2000c7b3)/customers`.

As the response, we have a complete list of our customers:

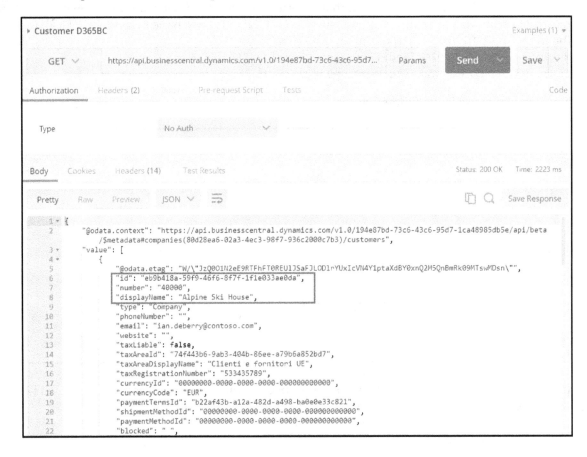

Now, we want to create a customer by using the API. We need to create a POST request to the following URL with `Content-Type = application/json`: `https://api.businesscentral.dynamics.com/v1.0/194e87bd-73c6-43c6-95d7-1ca48985db5e/api/beta/companies(80d28ea6-02a3-4ec3-98f7-936c2000c7b3)/customers`.

In the request body, we pass the following JSON code:

```
▸ Customer Create D365BC

POST ∨    https://api.businesscentral.dynamics.com/v1.0/194e87bd-73c6-43c6-95d7-1ca48985db5e/api/beta/companies(80d28ea6-02a3-4ec3-98f7-9...

Authorization ●    headers (2)    Body ●    Pre-request Script    Tests

● form-data    ● x-www-form-urlencoded    ● raw    ● binary    JSON (application/json) ∨

 1 ▾ {
 2         "displayName": "Stefano Demiliani",
 3         "type": "Company",
 4         "phoneNumber": "3334455",
 5         "email": "demiliani@outlook.com",
 6         "website": "www.demiliani.com",
 7         "taxLiable": false,
 8         "currencyId": "00000000-0000-0000-0000-000000000000",
 9         "currencyCode": "EUR",
10         "blocked": " ",
11         "balance": 0,
12         "overdueAmount": 0,
13         "totalSalesExcludingTax": 0,
14 ▾      "address": {
15             "street": "Viale Kennedy 87",
16             "city": "Borgomanero",
17             "state": "Italy",
18             "countryLetterCode": "IT",
19             "postalCode": "IT-28021"
20         }
21    }
```

After invoking the POST HTTP request, this is the response we have (the customer is created and we have the GUID and the Customer-assigned code):

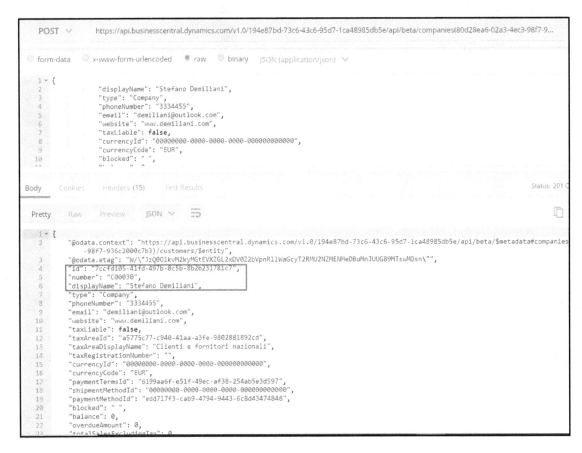

This is the customer record created in Dynamics 365 Business Central:

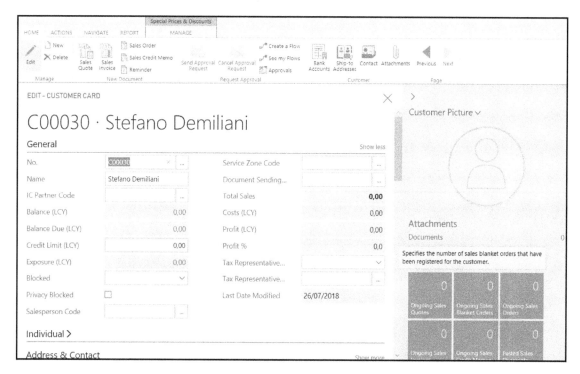

If we want to update some details of the previously created Customer by using the API (for example, the phone number), we can send an HTTP PATCH message (with `Content-Type = application/json`) to the following URL (passing the Customer GUID to update):

```
https://api.businesscentral.dynamics.com/v1.0/194e87bd-73c6-43c6-95d7-
1ca48985db5e/api/beta/companies(80d28ea6-02a3-4ec3-98f7-936c2000c7b3)/
customers(7ccfd105-41fd-497b-8c5b-8b2b231781c7).
```

The request body is as follows:

This is the obtained response:

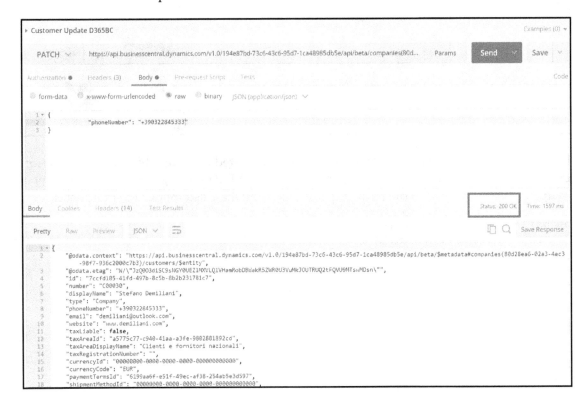

In Dynamics 365 Business Central, the phone number is updated accordingly:

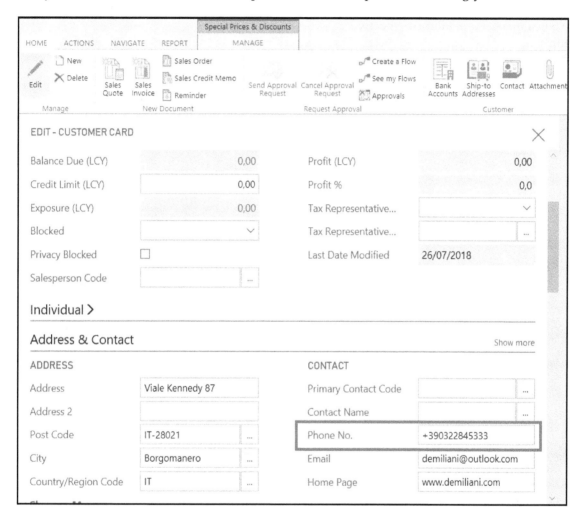

We can also apply filters in the query string. For example, to retrieve all Items with *Unit Price > 100*, you can perform a GET call to the following

URL: `http://api.businesscentral.dynamics.com/v1.0/194e87bd-73c6-43c6-95d7-1ca48985db5e/api/beta/companies(80d28ea6-02a3-4ec3-98f7-936c2000c7b3)/items`**?$filter=unitPrice%20gt%20100**.

REST APIs also support expansions, where in a single call you can retrieve an item and the related sub-items. For example, here we perform a GET call where we retrieve the details of a Sales Invoice and all the respective lines: `http://api.businesscentral.dynamics.com/v1.0/194e87bd-73c6-43c6-95d7-1ca48985db5e/api/beta/companies(80d28ea6-02a3-4ec3-98f7-936c2000c7b3)/salesInvoices(034a122b-962b-4007-b3d1-00718c2f21ff)?`**$expand=**`salesInvoiceLines`.

In the response, we have JSON with the `Sales Invoice` **Header** details:

In the same JSON for each Sales Header, we also have the **Lines** details:

As you can see, APIs are very powerful and a very performant way to integrate with Dynamics 365 Business Central by using simple HTTP methods (which is RESTful).

# DotNet variables

In the on-premise Microsoft Dynamics NAV world, many integrations with external applications are performed by using `DotNet` add-ins. The use of `DotNet` variables in Microsoft Dynamics 365 Business Central in the cloud (SaaS version) is actually not supported.

You can use `DotNet` variables only if your extension targets the on-premises version of Microsoft Dynamics 365 Business Central. For this, you have to set `"target"`: `"Internal"` in your `app.json` file in Visual Studio Code:

```
{} app.json    ✕

 2      "id": "73cd9423-1c38-4737-9e05-a578791bb906",
 3      "name": "DotNetTest",
 4      "publisher": "SD",
 5      "brief": "",
 6      "description": "",
 7      "version": "1.0.0.0",
 8      "privacyStatement": "",
 9      "EULA": "",
10      "help": "",
11      "url": "",
12      "logo": "",
13      "capabilities": [],
14      "dependencies": [],
15      "screenshots": [],
16      "platform": "11.0.0.0",
17      "application": "11.0.0.0",
18      "idRange": {
19        "from": 50100,
20        "to": 50149
21      },
22      "runtime": "Latest",
23      "target": "Internal"
24    }
```

A .NET type in the AL language is declared in the following way:

```
dotnet
{
    assembly(ASSEMBLY_NAME)
    {
        type(DOTNET_TYPE; ALIAS){}
    }
}
```

In preceding code, we can see the following:

- ASSEMBLY_NAME is the name of the assembly to reference
- DOTNET_TYPE is the .NET type to reference in the selected assembly (fully qualified name)
- ALIAS is an alias used to reference the .NET type from the AL code

When using DotNet from AL, you need to provide to Visual Studio Code, and to the AL compiler, the paths on which to search for the assemblies. As the default, the compiler knows only the mscorlib assembly location.

To do this, you need to go to your **User** or **Workspace** settings in Visual Studio Code (**File |Preferences | Settings**) and add the al.assemblyProbingPaths setting:

```
USER SETTINGS        WORKSPACE SETTINGS

        Place your settings here to overwrite the Default Settings.
1    {
2         "git.ignoreMissingGitWarning": true,
3         "al.assemblyProbingPaths": [
4             "./.netpackages",
5             "c:/Windows/assembly/",
6             "C:/Program Files/Microsoft Dynamics NAV/110/Service/Add-ins",
7             "C:/DotNetAddins"
8         ],
9         "window.zoomLevel": 1
10   }
```

This is an example of how to use a DotNet add-in (or DotNet assembly) in an AL extension. This function receives the path of an external document (such as a PDF file) and prints it directly, with the standard application associated with the file type in Windows.

The complete AL code is as follows:

```
dotnet
{
    assembly(mscorlib)
    {
        type(System.DateTime; MyDateTime) { }
    }
    assembly(System)
    {
        type(System.Diagnostics.Process; Process) { }
```

```
            type(System.Diagnostics.ProcessStartInfo; ProcessStartInfo) { }
            type(System.Diagnostics.ProcessWindowStyle; ProcessWindowStyle) { }
    }
}

codeunit 50100 DotNetWrapper
{
    trigger OnRun()
    begin
    end;
    procedure PrintExternalDocument(Path: Text[100])
    begin
        if NOT CallDotNet(Path) then
            Error('Error on printing document %1. \\ERROR: %2', Path,
             GetLastErrorText());
    end;

    [TryFunction]
    local procedure CallDotNet(Path: Text[100])

    var
        Process: DotNet Process;
        ProcessStartInfo: DotNet ProcessStartInfo;
        ProcessWindowStyle: DotNet ProcessWindowStyle;
    begin
        ProcessStartInfo := ProcessStartInfo.ProcessStartInfo(Path);
        ProcessStartInfo.Verb := 'Print';
        ProcessStartInfo.CreateNoWindow := true;
        ProcessStartInfo.WindowStyle := ProcessWindowStyle.Hidden;
        Process.Start(ProcessStartInfo);
    end;
}
```

# Azure Functions

**Azure Functions** is a serverless compute service offered by the Azure platform for running on-demand and event-driven code in the cloud. Azure Functions are actually the only way to run .NET code in the Dynamics 365 Business Central cloud platform (SaaS).

You can use an Azure Functions to migrate your existing on-premises .NET code to the cloud. An Azure Functions can be written directly via the Azure Portal (**Create a Resource | Function App**) or by using Visual Studio (with the Azure development tools installed). This second way is the recommended way if you want to have intellisense and automatic deployment.

To start creating an Azure Functions with Visual Studio, start a new project and select **Cloud | Azure Functions**, give a name to your project, and click **OK**.

You can now select **Azure Functions v1 (.NET Framework)** or **Azure Functions v2 Preview (.NET Standard)**. Here, we select the v1 version (v2 is for .NET Core and it's currently in preview).

Now Visual Studio asks you to choose a template for your Azure Function:

The available templates are the following:

- **Http Trigger**: Triggers the function execution by using an HTTP request
- **Blob Trigger**: Triggers the function execution when a blob is added to an Azure Storage container
- **Queue Trigger**: Triggers the function execution when a message arrives in an Azure Storage queue
- **Timer Trigger**: Triggers the function execution at a predefined schedule

We select **Http Trigger** and click **OK**. Visual Studio creates the project.

In this example, we have a function that receives a parameter name in the query string and, if correctly invoked, returns a message to the caller with the given name.

The Azure Function code is as follows:

```
public static class D365BCWorkshopFunction
    {
        [FunctionName("D365BCWorkshopFunction")]
        public static IActionResult
Run([HttpTrigger(AuthorizationLevel.Anonymous, "get", "post", Route =
null)]HttpRequest req, TraceWriter log)
        {
            log.Info("C# HTTP trigger function processed a request.");
            string name = req.Query["name"];
            string requestBody = new
            StreamReader(req.Body).ReadToEnd();
            dynamic data = JsonConvert.DeserializeObject(requestBody);
            name = name ?? data?.name;
            return name != null
                ? (ActionResult)new OkObjectResult($"Hello from Azure
                  Function (MS Workshop D365BC), {name}")
                : new BadRequestObjectResult("Please pass a name on the
                  query string or in the request body");
        }
    }
```

To publish our Azure Functions to the Azure cloud, just right-click on our project and select **Publish**.

You have to follow the publishing wizard and select your Azure subscription for creating the App Service where the function will be stored. When the publishing process is complete and all resources are provisioned, you can see the created resources in your Azure subscription and you have a public URL for calling your Azure Function:

| | D365BCWorkshopFunction | Application Insights | D365BCWorkshop | West Europe |
|---|---|---|---|---|
| | d365bcworkshopfunction | Storage account | D365BCWorkshop | West Europe |
| | D365BCWorkshopFunction | App Service | D365BCWorkshop | West Europe |

Here is an example of how you can call this Azure Function via AL code in an extension:

```
codeunit 50106 "AzureFunctionManagement"
{
    trigger OnRun()
    begin
    end;
    procedure CallAzureFunction(message: Text)
    var
        Client: HttpClient;
        Content: HttpContent;
        Response: HttpResponseMessage;
        stringContent: Text;
    begin
Client.Get('http://d365bcworkshopfunction.azurewebsites.net/api/d365bcworks
hopfunction?name=' + message, Response);
        Response.Content().ReadAs(stringContent);
        message('Output from Azure Function: ' + stringContent);
    end;
}
```

Here, we use the `HttpClient` AL object to send a GET HTPP request to the Azure Function URL passing the *name* parameter. Then, we read the response content and print the returned value.

Obviously, your function could be more complicated. It could, for example, load data from an external source and then return a complex object as a JSON response (imagine a function that, when triggered from Dynamics 365 Business Central, returns all orders collected from an external software or website, such as JSON).

This is a quick example of how to handle a JSON response message in an AL extension (the final code is not provided here):

```
codeunit 50105 B2BOrderManagement
{
    procedure LoadB2BOrders();
```

```
    var
        B2BOrders: Record B2B_Orders; //custom table for saving the
        received orders
        HttpClient: HttpClient;
        ResponseMessage: HttpResponseMessage;
        JsonToken: JsonToken;
        JsonValue: JsonValue;
        JsonObject: JsonObject;
        JsonArray: JsonArray;
        JsonText: text;
        i: Integer;
    begin
        // Call the Azure Function for retrieving the orders
        if not
    HttpClient.Get('https://B2BOrderRetrieva.azurewebsites.net',
    ResponseMessage)
        then
            Error('The call to the web service failed.');
        if not ResponseMessage.IsSuccessStatusCode then
            error('The web service returned an error message:\\' +
                'Status code: %1\' +
                'Description: %2',
                ResponseMessage.HttpStatusCode,
                ResponseMessage.ReasonPhrase);
        ResponseMessage.Content.ReadAs(JsonText);
        // Process JSON response
        if not JsonArray.ReadFrom(JsonText) then
        object');
        for i := 0 to JsonArray.Count - 1 do begin
            JsonArray.Get(i, JsonToken);
            JsonObject := JsonToken.AsObject;
            B2BOrders.init;
            if not JsonObject.Get('id', JsonToken) then
                error('Could not find a token with key %1');
            B2BOrders.id := JsonToken.AsValue.AsCode;
            B2BOrders.item := GetJsonToken(JsonObject,
            'item').AsValue.AsInteger;
            B2BOrders.qty := GetJsonToken(JsonObject,
            'qty').AsValue.AsDecimal();
            B2BOrders.order_date :=
            GetJsonToken(JsonObject,'order_date').AsValue.AsDateTime;
            B2BOrders.customer := SelectJsonToken(JsonObject,
            'customer').AsValue.AsText;
            B2BOrders.Insert;
        end;
    end;

    procedure GetJsonToken(JsonObject: JsonObject; TokenKey: text)
```

```
        JsonToken: JsonToken;
    begin
        if not JsonObject.Get(TokenKey, JsonToken) then
            Error('Could not find a token with key %1', TokenKey);
    end;

    procedure SelectJsonToken(JsonObject: JsonObject; Path: text)
        JsonToken: JsonToken;
    begin
        if not JsonObject.SelectToken(Path, JsonToken) then
            Error('Could not find a token with path %1', Path);
    end;
}
```

You can also POST a JSON request to an Azure Function from Dynamics 365 Business Central. Imagine a scenario where you have to POST all the Sales Orders created on the current day to an external application and your external application wants a JSON message with your Sales Order data constructed in a particular format. Here a quick example of how to create a JSON file in AL:

```
codeunit 50107 "PostJSONOrders"
{
    procedure CreateJsonOrder(): Text
    var
        JsonObjectHeader: JsonObject;
        JsonObjectLines: JsonObject;
        JsonArray: JsonArray;
        JsonArrayLines: JsonArray;
        SalesHeader: Record "Sales Header";
        SalesLines: Record "Sales Line";
        JsonText: Text;
    begin
        // Loops through the Sales Header
        SalesHeader.SetRange("Document Type", SalesHeader."Document
         Type"::Order);
        SalesHeader.SetRange("Order Date", Today());
        if SalesHeader.FindSet() then
            repeat
                //JSON Header data
                JsonObjectHeader.Add('Sales Order No.',
                SalesHeader."No.");
                JsonObjectHeader.Add('Bill-to Name', SalesHeader."Bill-
                to Name");
                JsonObjectHeader.Add('Order Date', SalesHeader."Order
                 Date");
                JsonArray.Add(JsonObjectHeader);
                //Loop through Lines
                SalesLines.SetRange("Document Type",
```

```
        SalesLines."Document Type"::Order);
        SalesLines.SetRange("Document No.", SalesHeader."No.");
        // JsonObject Initialization
        JsonObjectLines.Add('Line No.', '');
        JsonObjectLines.Add('Item No.', '');
        JsonObjectLines.Add('Location Code', '');
        JsonObjectLines.Add('Quantity', '');
        if SalesLines.FindSet() then
            repeat
                //JSON line data
                JsonObjectLines.Replace('Line No.',
                 SalesLines."Line No.");
                JsonObjectLines.Replace('Item No.',
                 SalesLines."No.");
                JsonObjectLines.Replace('Location Code',
                 SalesLines."Location Code");
                JsonObjectLines.Replace('Quantity',
                  SalesLines.Quantity);
                JsonArrayLines.Add(JsonObjectLines);
            until SalesLines.Next() = 0;
        JsonArray.Add(JsonArrayLines);
    until SalesHeader.Next() = 0;
    //Returns the JSON text to the caller
    JsonArray.WriteTo(JsonText);
    exit(JsonText);
  end;
}
```

Here, this function creates a JSON file with the order details and this JSON is returned as a Text value. Then you can call an Azure Function or another web service and POST this JSON message.

# Microsoft Flow

**Microsoft Flow** is a cloud-based workflow service that permits you to create automated processes across multiple applications without writing any lines of code.

To start using Microsoft Flow with Dynamics 365 Business Central, log in to `https://flow.microsoft.com/` and search for Business Central. Here are the available flows:

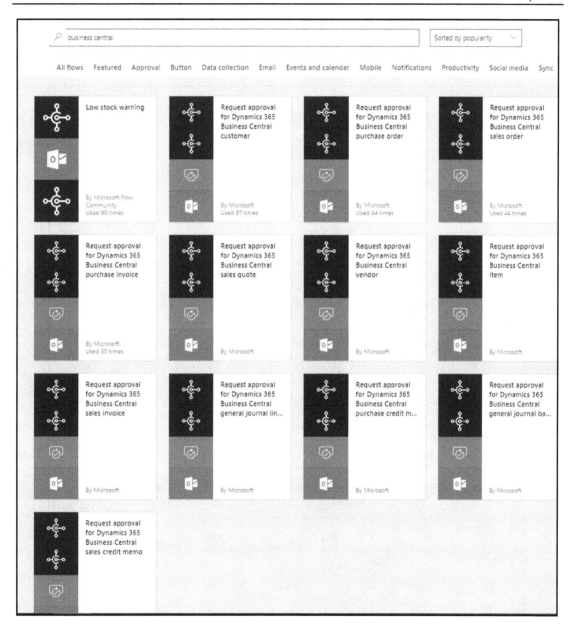

To create a new workflow, select one of the available templates (here I've selected the *Request approval for Dynamics 365 Business Central Sales Order* template).

When selected, a wizard starts. It first shows the connected accounts (Dynamics 365 Business Central Office 365), and in the next window, you can graphically compose your flow by inserting the workflow parameters:

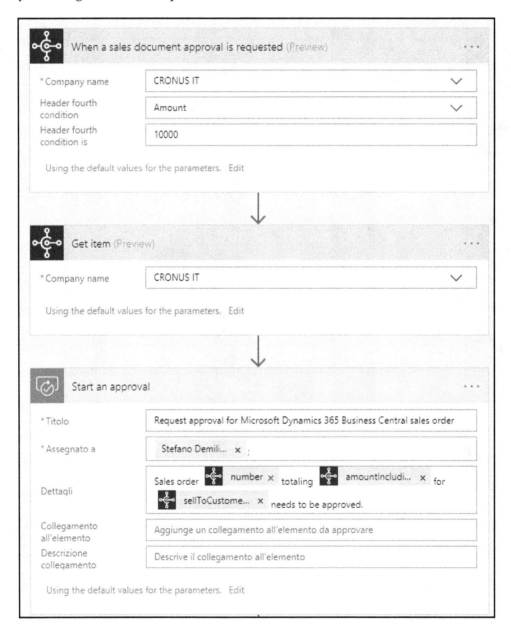

Then you can insert the conditions:

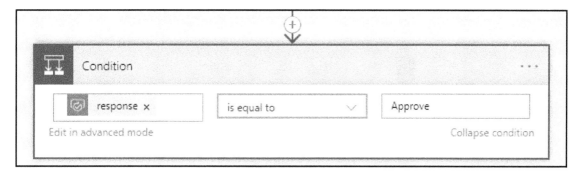

If the order is approved, an email is sent to the order creator:

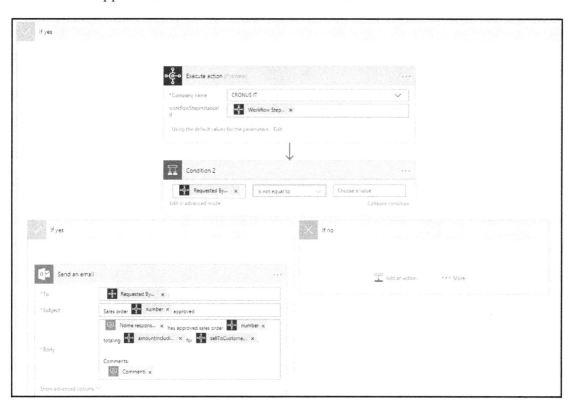

If the order is not approved, a different notification email is sent to the order approval:

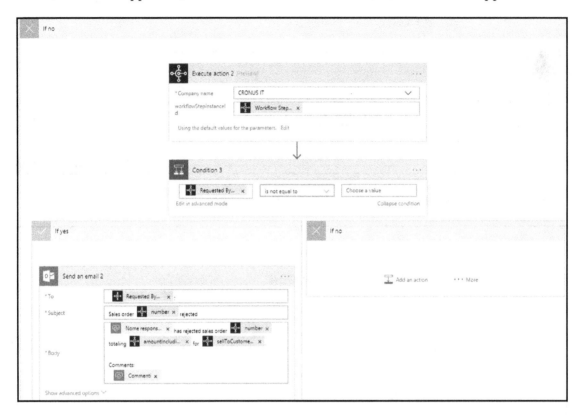

Obviously, you can customize this flow as you want to satisfy your business needs, but this is outside the scope of this book.

For more information regarding **Microsoft Flow**, check out the following links:

- https://docs.microsoft.com/en-us/flow/
- https://docs.microsoft.com/en-us/flow/getting-started
- https://docs.microsoft.com/en-us/flow/guided-learning/

# Microsoft PowerApps

Microsoft PowerApps is a cloud-based and no-code solution offered by the Office 365 platform to create web- and mobile-data-connected applications.

To create a PowerApps connected to Dynamics 365 Business Central, log in to `https://powerapps.microsoft.com/`, select the Apps menu on the left, and then click on **Create an App**:

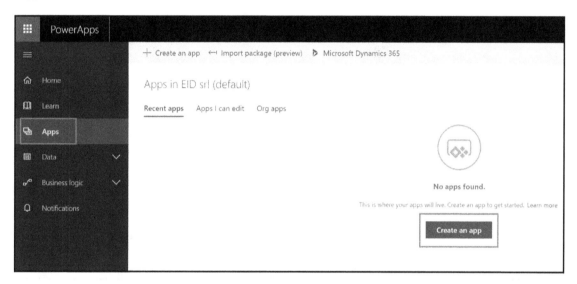

In the Connection menu, select **Microsoft Dynamics 365 Business Central** and then click **Create**. A wizard will create a connection to your Dynamics 365 Business Central tenant.

Now you can choose a dataset to work with (selected from the list of your companies), select a table (from all the tables published as OData web services in Dynamics 365 Business Central), and click **Connect**:

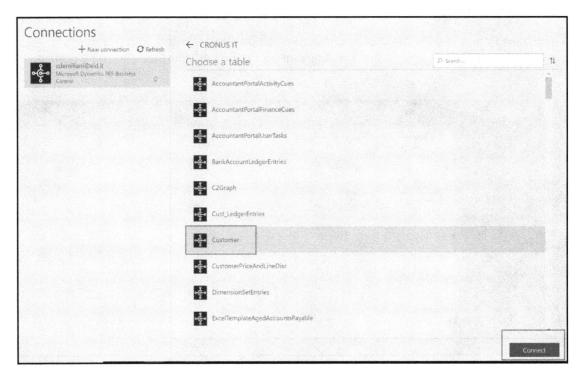

PowerApps creates a connection to your data, and after few seconds **PowerApps Studio** is started. Here is the place where you can start building your app:

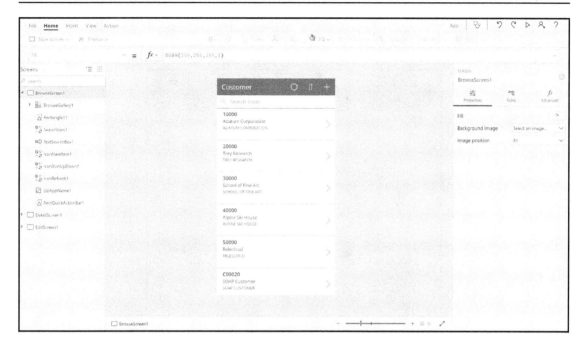

The PowerApps Studio

You can customize the layout, add more fields to the app pages, and many other things:

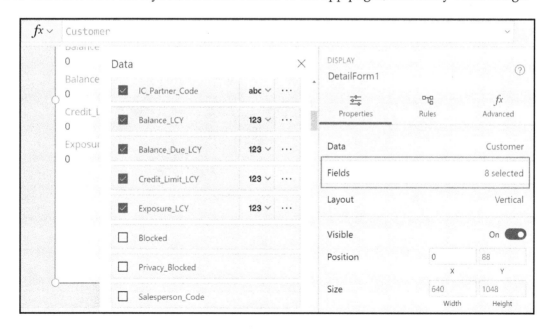

If we just start this app (where we've written zero lines of code), we have a mobile app that lists our Dynamics 365 Business Central Customers:

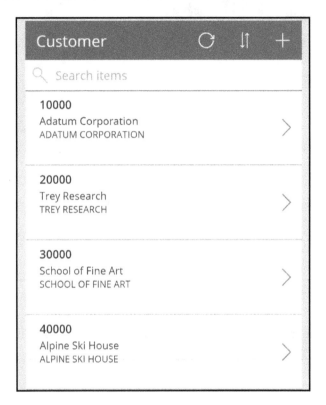

We can immediately filter the list of customers using a search box:

If we click on a customer, we can see their details (they are totally customizable) and we can edit them:

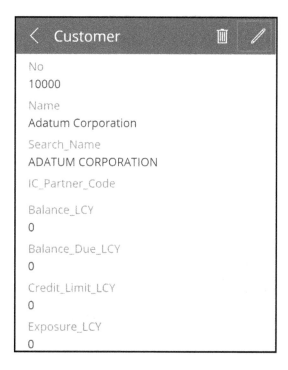

When we save the modifications, a query is sent to our Dynamics 365 Business Central tenant and the record is updated accordingly.

When your app is finished, you can save it on PowerApps.com (`https://powerapps.microsoft.com/en-us/`) or locally:

Then you can share the app in your organization (with the entire organization or only with specific members) with the desired permissions:

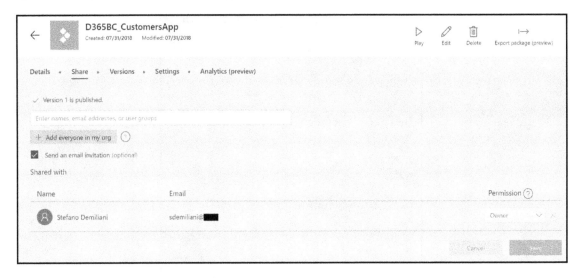

After saving the publishing operation, your app is ready to be used in your organization.

You can find more information about Microsoft PowerApps at `https://powerapps.microsoft.com/`.

# Summary

In this chapter, we saw how we can integrate Dynamics 365 Business Central with external applications by using APIs and web services. We learned how to use Azure Functions (for SaaS) and DotNet assemblies (for on-premise) to extend Dynamics 365 Business Central. Then, we looked at how to create serverless processes and applications with Dynamics 365 Business Central using Azure Function, Flow, and PowerApps.

By the end of this book, you'll be ready to master Dynamics 365 Business Central Development.

# Other Books You May Enjoy

If you enjoyed this book, you may be interested in these other books by Packt:

**Implementing Azure Cloud Design Patterns**
Oliver Michalski, Stefano Demiliani

ISBN: 978-1-78839-336-2

- Learn to organize Azure access
- Design the core areas of the Azure Execution Model
- Work with storage and data management
- Create a health endpoint monitoring pattern
- Automate early detection of anomalies
- Identify and secure Azure features

## Building ERP Solutions with Microsoft Dynamics NAV
Stefano Demiliani

ISBN: 978-1-78712-308-3

- Configure NAV Web Services and create external applications with Visual Studio, .NET, and .NET Core
- Solve technical architectural problems by implementing enterprise solutions with NAV
- Develop applications and solutions with Microsoft Dynamics NAV and the Microsoft technology stack
- Create a Power BI dashboard for rich reporting and NAV data analysis
- Find out how to transmit your device location from a UWP application to NAV in order to implement a distributed solution for managing couriers in a sales company
- Make the most of Microsoft Azure and its services
- Create enterprise solutions with NAV by using Azure App Service
- Use Azure Service Bus for managing distributed NAV applications

# Leave a review - let other readers know what you think

Please share your thoughts on this book with others by leaving a review on the site that you bought it from. If you purchased the book from Amazon, please leave us an honest review on this book's Amazon page. This is vital so that other potential readers can see and use your unbiased opinion to make purchasing decisions, we can understand what our customers think about our products, and our authors can see your feedback on the title that they have worked with Packt to create. It will only take a few minutes of your time, but is valuable to other potential customers, our authors, and Packt. Thank you!

# Index

developing, for extension 125, 127, 128
Customer Relationship Management (CRM) 7

# D

DotNet variables
  using 185, 186, 187
Dynamics 365 Business Central
  REST APIs 175, 177, 179, 181, 183, 184, 185
  web services 170, 171, 173, 174
dynamics translation service (DTS) 121

# E

Enterprise Resource Planning (ERP) 7
ERP cloud-based version
  Microsoft Dynamics 365 Business Central 8
  Microsoft Dynamics 365 for Financials &
    Operations 8
events, in Microsoft Dynamics NAV
  event 33
  publisher 33
  subscriber 33
events
  about 33
  business events 34
  database events 34
  global events 34
  integration events 34
  page events 34
extension deployment
  about 137
  automatic deployment 138, 139, 141
  manual deployment 158, 159
  semi-automatic deployment 141, 142, 143, 145,
    146, 147, 149, 150, 152
extension
  about 37
  custom business logic (Codeunit), writing 109,
    110, 112, 113, 115, 116, 117
  custom report, developing 125, 127, 128
  dependency 128, 130, 131
  developing 89
  developing, with AL language 55
  pages, creating for new tables 96, 97, 99, 101
  standard Dynamics 365 Business Central
    Objects, extending 103, 104, 105, 106, 108

tables, creating 90, 92, 94, 96

# F

Financial Object (FOB) 39

# G

general availability (GA) 14
General Data Protection Regulation (GDPR) 21
Git
  native AL source-code management 62

# H

Headline
  about 122
  customizing 122, 123, 124
HelloWorld.al sample 58, 59

# I

independent software vendor (ISV) 48
Independent Software Vendors (ISVs) 18
integrated development environment (IDE) 28
intellectual property (IP) 162
Intellectual Property (IP) 15

# L

local-hosted sandbox 76, 78, 79
locally hosted Dynamics 365 Business Central
  sandbox
  creating 81, 82, 83

# M

Managed Service for Partners (MSfP)
  reference 15
manual deployment
  of extension 158, 159
Microsoft Dynamics 365 Business Central
  Licensing Guide
  reference 9
Microsoft Dynamics 365 Business Central Web
  Client
  supported browsers 10
Microsoft Dynamics 365 Business Central
  about 7, 8, 10, 11
  architecture 18

standard Dynamics 365 Business Central Objects
   extending 103, 104, 105, 106, 108
Sync-NAVApp
   reference 143

## T

traditional Microsoft Dynamics NAV customizations 27, 28, 29, 30, 31
translations
   handling, with XLIFF files 118, 119, 120, 121
triggers 32

## U

user experience (UX) 153

## V

Value Added Resellers (VARs) 18
Visual Studio Code debugger
   reference 160
Visual Studio Code workspace
   anatomy 49

Code Editor 51
Menu bar 50
Side bar 51
Status bar 51
View bar 50
Visual Studio Code
   advantages 48
   characteristics 48
   support, to Git 63, 64
   tips 52
   versus CSIDE (Client Server Integrated Development Environment) 53

## W

worldwide standard application base 11

## X

XLIFF files
   reference 121
   translations, handling 118, 119, 120, 121
XML Localization Interchange File Format (XLIFF) 43